An Anthology Of Christ's Teachings

FRED G MACKAMAN

ISBN 979-8-89526-550-5 (paperback)
ISBN 979-8-89526-551-2 (digital)

Christian Faith Publishing
832 Park Avenue
Meadville, PA 16335
www.christianfaithpublishing.com

Printed in the United States of America

PREFACE

There is a continuity in all of Jesus' Teachings. The contents of this book is just the beginning. Learning never stops and has no end.

We are forever grateful to Our God that He Loves us so much and is infinitely interested in our development as Loving and Obedient Sons and Daughters.

All these Teachings are directly from God to prepare us for His Coming. To learn to live the Life that He has ordained for us.

THREE BOOKS OF CHRIST'S TEACHINGS

- **<u>Living In God</u>**

- **<u>Let Go And Let God</u>**

- **<u>Everything Happens For A Purpose</u>**

LIVING IN GOD

My Story

FREDERICK G MACKAMAN

CONTENTS

Section I.

- INTRODUCTION..1

Section II.

- Hearing God's Voice...3
- My Role and Obedience to God's Will.................................3
    God's Spirit Has Been Given to Me...............................4
    My Training And Instruction 5
    Indicators Given To Me For Affirmation Of My Faith......6
- Total Surrender To God..7
- The Purpose Of Life - God's Plan....................................7
- My Life In Christ...8

Section III.

- Called By God - Be My Scribe and Messenger.....................10
- Conversion Experience..12
- Who Are Charismatic Christians.......................................12
    What Are Some Of The Unique Practices Of
    The Charismatic Christians...13
    Why Become A Charismatic Christian?.........................14
    How Does One Become A Charismatic Christian?.........14

Section IV.

- We Are Unique 15
- How We Become Different 15
- Why Did God Create Us...15
- Adam and Eve – Our Downfall 17

Section V.

- Pursuit Of Truth...18
- Where Do You Go To Get Your Truth?.................................19
- What Does Webster Say About Truth?................................19
- My Personal Definition Of Truth Is The Following: 19
- People Disagree With The Meaning Of Truth. Why Is This? ...19
- Why Do We Need Truth?..20
- Our Form Of Government..21
- Where Do You Get Your Truth? 22
- Truth Is Critical In Life 23

Section VI.

- What Is A Man And What Is A Woman................................24
  - Some Key Characteristics of a Man 24
  - Some key Characteristics of Women................................24
- What Is A Woman 24
- MARRIAGE AND DIVORCE...25
- In Marriage - You Are Right 26
- Sexual Component In God's Love 27

Section VII.

- A SERIES OF MIRACLES 27
- My Life Story of Miracles Begins.......................................28
- My Early Life 29
- My Life In The Army 29
- A Very Unusual Miracle 31

Section VIII.

- Our Destiny Depends Upon Us 31

Life's Lessons

- Padre Pio's Affect On Me..33

ADDENDUM:

Additional Graces, Gifts, and Promises From God

- Life Is The Answer 34
- Our Human Nature 35
- Understanding Unbelievers 36
- You Become What You Think About.....................36
- My Proclamation - God's Word............................37
- The Power Of Self 37
- The Lord's Plan 37
- Everything Happens For A Purpose.......................38
- Journey To Innermost God...................................38
- Total Surrender To God..39
- To Gain Access To The Lord 39
- God Is The Only True Reality 40
- God Is Always The Same......................................41
- God's Word Defined 42
- God's Grace For Us His Children 42
- God's Gifts To Us - Our Prayers To Him 43
- For Love Of God...43
- Let Go And Let God 44
- Prayer To God 45
- God Is Infinite 46
- Who Is A Christian 46
- Accessing The Inner Self......................................47
- The Spirit Of Fire..48
- Release Of The Holy Spirit...................................48
- The Holy Spirit Consists Of:................................49
- Focus On God Continuously 49
- Understanding Prophecy From God: Release of
  the Holy Spirit 49
- God's Methods Of Teaching His Word..................50
- Today Is All We Have...50
- Lessons In Life 50
- When Events Do Not Transpire As Expected.........51

–   God's Love And Gifts To His Children 51
–   My Experience With God And My Father......................51
–   Satan's Agenda And Methods 52
–   There Is Only One God 52
–   Satan Controls Us Through What We Love....................53

CONCLUSION 54

INTRODUCTION

These **Words** are from the Holy Spirit, the third person of God. They come to me primarily while I am praying my rosaries during the day. I either stop and write them immediately or place them on notes to be recorded later. I am assisted by the Holy Spirit with the wording when I write them.

"I live for the **Word of God** and the **Teachings of Jesus.**" These are **My Truth.**

I have been a Christian since 8-years old. I converted and became a disciple of Jesus in the Assembly of God Church during Daily Vacation Bible School. I was not baptized. I have lived according to the principles taught by Jesus ever since.

My birth mother died of influenza when I was 3-years old. In those days fathers did not raise their children independently. My dad was taking me to work with him and to restaurants to eat. I could not eat after my mother's death. In a restaurant my dad was trying to get me to eat. A young lady 19-years old said, "I can get him to eat," and she did. I immediately started calling her, "muvver." My dad hired her as a full-time housekeeper who lived with us. Not too long after this they were married. My dad was 44-years old. Many years later in my life, my mother told me that she married my dad so she could raise me. The first of many miracles in my life.

My dad died when I was 14-years old. He had divorced my mother when I was twelve, and I was living with him. The judge at the hearing granted custody to my mother's family as she had married again by this time. So, I stayed with my grandmother, grandfather, and two uncles. One of the uncles was an Assembly of God minister and ministered to the farm workers.

That was a perfect environment for a teenager to be in; a very spiritual family to show me how to live. I flourished, spiritually. Another major miracle.

In my several careers I have always been moved ahead of others and rewarded with so many gifts and achievements that it is truly amazing.

My entire life has been blessed with many miracles. I am certain everyone has similar experiences if they just recognize them.

This brief account of my life is to illustrate the background that I have been given by God to prepare me for the **Mission** He has given to me.

This **Mission,** which He told me when He brought me into His Church, the Holy Catholic Church which Jesus Founded, was to be, a **Scribe and a Messenger.**

This document was dictated to me by the Holy Spirit in order to convey God's Message to the world. Most of the revelations were given to me while praying my rosaries. The Holy Spirit has directed me to pray the entire rosary, 20-decades, every day. I am so humbled that He would entrust this task to me. When I ask God, "Why me?" His response is always the same, "If not you, then who."

Hearing God's Voice

Let us begin with the hearing of The Lord God's Voice.

We hear voices in our head constantly, and we think they are our thoughts. There are only two sources of original thought. You may believe those are our thoughts, but they are not. We cannot generate something from nothing. Original thought is either from God, or from The Evil One, Satan. When questioned on this, God revealed to me the true test is, *"If the idea results in good, then it is from Me, if the results lead to evil, then they are from The Evil One."* This made sense to me.

We can take these thoughts and manipulate them with our own life experiences and come to any number of conclusions. Frequently, we mislead ourselves with our false reasoning. It is so easy to continue down this path with an active mind.

If you listen to God, Our Creator, He wants to Help us in everything, even down to the smallest details.

Let Him Help! Our God is constantly waiting for us.

My Role and Obedience to God's Will

"I exist at the **Pleasure of God**."

The **Definition of Faith** given to me by the Holy Spirit: "**Knowledge of, and Obedience to, the Holy Spirit**, The Third Person of God."

Every morning, and night, one of my prayers is to **Surrender My Will** to **My God** and request that He replace it with **His Will**. I want to understand, and follow His Will in everything I do, and not follow any other path.

During my earlier times in His Church, I would be awakened by the Holy Spirit at 2:30 in the morning to perform my nightly prayers. One night, after this ritual, the Holy Spirit summoned me to get up and pray again. I responded with, "Lord, I was just up to pray." He repeated, "Get up and Pray." So, I did. As I kneeled, God told me, **"I am Placing you in My Heart!"** A very safe and Holy Place to reside.

Also, early on with my intimate experience with Our Lord God, I sought a Spiritual Advisor. As I continued in this pursuit, The Holy Spirit informed me, "Why are you looking for an advisor while **I am directly communicating with you**?"

Thus far I have been given two visions. I believe these were to strengthen my faith. The first occurred while I was laying on my bed during the afternoon. I was taken to a mountain slope in Heaven, and on a grassy slope with large boulders protruding from the surface. There were many cats, probably thirty or so, on and around these boulders. They all were ecstatic to see me. I petted them and we all shared in God's Love. I assumed they were all the cats that I had petted during my lifetime. This vision lasted about two to three minutes, then was gone. During this entire time, I had the constant, very strong emotion of **Euphoria**! The definition of euphoria is, "Intense Joy."

The second vision occurred just after we had to put down LUV, one of our two cats, due to cancer. She was especially beloved by both me and my wife. My wife and I were sitting in our living area in our apartment. This vision was only for me. Jesus, Himself, was to my right where the bookcase and TV were placed normally. He was petting LUV as she was stretched out laying on her tummy. As Jesus was stroking her, He said to me, "You can visit her anytime you wish." I assumed that He meant after I was in Heaven, but I was not certain of this. Perhaps I could visit her now. I would really like to do that, but how would I accomplish it?

God's Spirit Has Been Given to Me

I have experienced several healings of others, granted by Our God, through me as His Instrument. All this falls within His mandate for me as His Servant.

The very first, when He called me to His Church, was for our assistant charismatic leader. She had asthma attacks several times a year. Usually, she would have to be hospitalized a couple of times a year. The Holy Spirit directed me to sit her in a chair directly in front of the tabernacle where the Holy Prescence is kept and pray for her. As I did this, I was joined by a few women in my prayers over her. I was further instructed to stand behind her and place my hands on her head. I had already experienced the fact that when the Holy Spirit is on me, I tear up copiously. While I prayed over her, my tears drenched her head and she was **Healed**, not from my tears, but by the prayers to the Holy Spirit. She never experienced asthma again! She was so happy that she sent me a three-year subscription to Magnificat Magazine and Father's Day cards for seven years!

A recent Healing in which the Holy Spirit used me was for a lady who sits nearby during daily Mass. She came to Mass with her right eye quite swollen and related that the doctor could not ascertain what was causing the swelling. Just before she left, I called the woman who sits behind me to assist in praying over her with hands on prayer. Jesus said, "When two or more pray in My Name, their prayer will be answered." When she came to mass the next day, her eye was completely healed!

The most recent healing was for David, a man who sits behind me during mass every day. His doctor told him that his infected toe would have to be removed. His wife, and another lady and I prayed over him with hands on and with tongues which came from me. His doctor informed him at his next visit that, "He had dodged the bullet," and his toe would not have to be removed.

My Training And Instruction

I was instructed by the Holy Spirit to **Read the Bible daily**. I have completed reading the Bible 8-times. The last 3-times, I have studied It, and read it only one chapter a day.

I attended the Diocese program of **Healing Prayer** which consists of 86-classroom hours. This program was so enjoyable that I didn't want it to end.

I Love the Catechism! It contains the answers to the questions about our beliefs as given by God. I wish all members of Jesus's Church would read it in its entirety. There is a program on the computer that presents a daily part, and if read daily, completes the entire Catechism within a year. I have done this twice.

I have attended the 2-year course on the Catechism which all teachers in Catholic Schools are required to attend, and **I have my signed Certificate of Attendance**. It consists of 86 classroom hours and homework along with it.

I love to sing and have sung for my own pleasure all my life. **I sang in the choir** for over 7 years until I could no longer attend the night practices.

I served as an Extraordinary Minister and served for several years until I became too unsteady to hold the wine chalice.

I love to serve as a Lector. I performed this role at my Church for a few years on Fridays until the school mass was moved there, and the students conducted the mass. I also served in this capacity at a sister church on Tuesdays for about a year until I could no longer do this.

I served on the Faith Formation for three years. I was not able to assume my role as leader when it became my turn.

<u>Indicators Given To Me For Affirmation Of My Faith</u>

During every Mass, as the Holy Body of Christ is raised and presented to God in Concentration to Him, **I see a hole in the middle of the Eucharist** about small finger sized. I do not know what this represents, but in my experience with Our Lord, the answer will be made apparent to me at some future time.

I have had several visions of images in the consecrated Hosts. The first was after I became a member of Jesus's Church, the Holy Catholic Church. One time it was with a dark background and shimmering colors of red, green, blue, etc. It took me a while to discern what this meant, but eventually I understood that it was my birthstone, the Opal for October. The Host looked like a giant, sparkling Opal!

Later, it became a solid line across the middle of the host. It varied in height according to where my spirituality was at the time! Also, the background was either dark due to recent thoughts and activities and changing to white as my prayers during adoration affected this color. A couple of my spiritual friends both see Jesus's Face in the Host, always.

<u>Total Surrender To God</u>

<u>Belief and Faith</u> cannot be explained; they can only be experienced by the giving up of Ones Self's Will and **<u>Surrendering it to God</u>**!

Do not be Confused. "**<u>There is Only One God!</u>**" There are many who are proclaimed, but there is only One Creator of All.

<u>I Am</u> He, who is above everything and the Creator of All!

There is **<u>Only One Truth</u>**! That is God's Truth, since He was The Creator of Everything that was Created.

Anything else comes from the Deceiver, the father of all lies, Satan who seeks to destroy what God has created.

Let us always remember, **Nothing Happens Unless God Creates It, or Allows It To Occur!** He is in **Control of Everything, Always!**

God causes some good to come out of all evil, and **He** allows evil to exist to test our response, and actions from our gift of Free Will. We determine events by our actions; **He** allows this and responds with **His Purpose!**

<u>The Purpose Of Life - God's Plan</u>

God created us, His children, in Love and for Love. He desired to have people to share His immense Love, and to include ones for His personal fellowship. Angels do His Will, but God desired spirits who could share True Love, Freely Given by the choice of Free Will.

For this reason, the gift of Free Will was necessary. To release this immense power into humanity is a risk. God determined, with His Perfect Knowledge, that this power must be tested before being released into existence. God uses the instrument of Satan for this purpose.

Satan can only do what God allows; therefore the testing is controlled. Recall that Satan was formerly Lucifer, the highest, the most beautiful, and the top ranked angel in heaven. Who else but him to be picked for this most important assignment?

For this program to be totally effective, Satan truly becomes this Character of Lucifer. He asks for help and takes one third of the angels in heaven to assist him in carrying out his new role as God's protagonist.

So we are all being tested for assurance that we will be totally obedient to Our God, which is Holiness. Anything less cannot be released into this universe or allowed to escape into higher levels of existence.

We tend to expect happiness and comfort for this life. God does give us consolations from time to time, but we are being tested, and this requires suffering. It is exceedingly difficult for us to understand the connection between love and suffering, but the saints understand and glory in it since they know that the suffering if for God's Love of us. Christ suffered on the cross for Love of us; we suffer with Him to attach ourselves to Our God.

<u>My Life In Christ</u>

My mother died when I was three years old, and my father died when I was fourteen.

I accepted Jesus as my personal Savior at an Assembly of God Daily Vacation Bible School meeting when I was 8-years old.

When my mother died, my dad could not get me to eat. A 19-year-old young lady said, "I can get him to eat," and she did! I called her "muvver," after that as I could not pronounce, "mother." My dad hired her as his housekeeper, and they were married soon after that. My dad was 44-years old. My new mother, Pauline, told me later in life that she married my dad just to raise me.

My dad divorced her to marry his business partner when I was twelve. When he died, I was placed with her family as she had remarried. God was working His Plan for me as this was a very holy family. My mother was a rebel and did not accept the faith, but my two uncles and Grandmother were very spiritual. One of the uncles was an ordained minister in the church and ministered to the farm workers. An ideal environment for a young, impressionable teenager. I was a willing subject! The treated me like a "young prince." I could do no wrong, and I reciprocated in love for them.

Everywhere I went in life, I was moved ahead of everyone else, in my work, in the Army where I served for 2-years, and in my work at IBM for over 34-years. I hired in at entry level and advanced to fourth level management before early retirement at 59- years of age. I spent most of my career managing new product releases and working with people. I love people, and people love me. I now know that is why I was so successful, as God was with me and blessed me constantly.

All of us managers went on frequent business trips. After the meetings of the day, we would go out to a nice dinner and afterwards we would sit at the bar and drink. There were no non-drinkers; we were all drinkers. Later, some could stop drinking, others could not quit. I was one of those. I suspect that with any addiction, there is a point where we do not have control of our actions; Satan has assumed control! I prayed and prayed but could not stop drinking! I suffered for 40-years. There was a time, early on, that when I was looking in my mirror at home in my bathroom. I looked at my face and God spoke to me directly, "If you stop drinking now, your memory will not be affected." Did I stop? Could I stop? I did not know, but I did not stop, so I suffered.

My company had moved us to Florida where we lived for 42-years. One night my wife noticed and said, "You are not drinking tonight!" I had not noticed! I took notice of what was happening. Suddenly, I could understand things I could never comprehend before; my mind expanded tremendously! Also, in subsequent days/ weeks, my hair went back to its normal color as it was turning gray. In fact, I had been deteriorating at a rapid rate and my wife, Charlotte had told me, "You will be dead in 6-months!" My age reversed and although I had always looked young for my age, my aging had reversed itself! My God at work again. His Plans were being implemented. I was seventy years old at the time, February 2002.

Three years and three months later, not before, and not at the same time, the next significant event occurred. On Mother's Day in May 2005, I went to The Catholic Church where my son and daughter-law were married. I went with them as I do with any of my children, I go with them to the church of their choice. As everyone was taking communion, I stood up to let them through. I thought to myself, "I am a Christian, should I take communion?" I asked Jesus, "Should I take communion?" His answer came back immediately, a resounding, "Yes!" So, I took communion. My eyes filled with overflowing tears; the floor was literally flooded where I took the Consecrated Host! I now know that when The Spirit is on me, I tear copiously. Soon thereafter, as we were walking down the steps of the church, in my head I told myself, "I could never join this church! Too much Ritual." Immediately a command voice came into my head, and said, "What do you mean? This is My Church and My Roots!" I was in the Army and I know a command voice when I hear it. It must be obeyed. In my mind I immediately snapped to attention and saluted. The very next morning I reported for duty to the Priest! He said we must get you baptized right away! He gave me a stack of books and I did nothing but read for two months. When he felt I was ready, He, personally conducted a full mass for my family and friends to baptize me, this on September 26, 2005. I was confirmed with the high school students on February 10, 2006 as I could not wait until Easter.

Called By God - Be My Scribe and Messenger

Three and a half years before I had my conversion experience, God gave me His Gift of Knowledge, Wisdom, and Power in His Name! This is the Holy Spirit! His Spirit!

I was a business drinker, drinking on business trips and later at home by myself; we all were that went on these business trips. My first encounter with God was one time I was looking at myself in my bathroom mirror and God spoke from my image of myself saying, "If you stop drinking now, it will not affect your memory." Did I stop? Could I stop? I do not know as I did not give this experience any credence at the time; it was just an occurrence. It took 40-years later, and a miracle from God to let me stop drinking!

That is my story of how He brought me to His Prescence.

One night my wife said, "You are not drinking tonight." I had not even noticed! I was 73-years old then, and my hair was turn-ing white and I could hardly walk 50-yards. My wife told me that I would be dead in 6-months at the rate I was going. But on this night, I was given a tremendous **Miracle.** My mind was expanded to an extent that I could understand so many things I could never understand before. My aging was reversed, and my hair began returning to its original color of light brown! My features also began looking younger. It was determined later that my mind was regressed to 32-years of age, and my body to be in the 50's. I was told later by the Holy Spirit that when people comment on my age, just tell that them you are ageless and eternal.

During this entire process, God told me, "You are a Scribe and a Messenger for Me." He has used me in large measure as a scribe to take dictation from His Spirit, and I cannot change a word or punctuation! It is Holy Writ!

At some later time, God asked me if I would be a sacrifice for Him? Without any hesitation, I answered YES!

At another time He asked if I would take on His wounds for Him? I hesitated since I knew all about Padre Pio's suffering. I had had the opportunity to pray over Padre Pio's gloves and had a special connection to him ever since. He helps me in my travails. Shortly after this, just after taking the Holy Body and Blood of our Savior, Jesus Christ, as I was kneeling, my right hand started to swell up with blood on the back of my hand! No puncture wound, just a massive swelling.

I took this as an aid to help me make up my mind of whether to accept God's offer, or not. Two weeks later I told God, "It is too much to bear." I have regretted this decision ever since, but there is no going back. At the time I was not aware that there are several in the world who bear His Wounds, but on a lesser scale, such as bleeding only on Thursdays!

My sorrow continues for I learned a strong lesson, Never refuse any offer from Our God; He always knows best!

In the not-too-distant past God has called me, "His Reluctant Apostle." He encourages me to speak out more forcefully and use the Power He has given me. At one time, a Holy One whom God used to speak to our Charismatic group, had a Word From God for me. It was, "Speak out more Forcefully!" I now speak out with greater confidence and knowledge of God Himself in His Spirit. I look to Him to help me develop into the person he planned and wants me to be.

<u>Conversion Experience</u>

God, Our Father, who created everything, created each one of us, His children. He loves us beyond all measure and treats each one of us as an only child. He gave us Free Will so our love for Him has meaning. For we must Choose Him to validate this love for Him as freely chosen and True Love, freely given.

He desires all our love for Him as Our Father which is His due. He prescribes that we show Him our love by Perfect Obedience to Him. He gave us Free Will to confirm our Love for Him. Only we can make this choice; no one, not even God Himself can make this decision for us. It must be Our Choice, freely given, to be valid True Love for Our God.

When we are conceived God, Our Father designs every aspect of us, our physical shape and characteristics, our personality, and our talents. He also gives us our strengths and weaknesses. He also gives us our spirit, which is from His Spirit.

He has a life plan for each of us and follows us in every thought, word, and action! He knows we have no life experience yet and that we must learn, grow, and advance to His Plan for us. We make mistakes, learn from them, and advance in knowledge.

At some point in our lives, we must meet Jesus, who is the Son of the Father. He came to earth to teach us how God instructed us to live. We must develop a one-on-one, personal relationship with Jesus, for then we will have a connection with God that will never be severed.

<u>Who Are Charismatic Christians</u>

Typically, Charismatic Christians are Catholics who are <u>Living In The Holy Spirit</u> as the early Church Fathers did. However, they do not share all of their possessions as was done then, but they practice all of the basic teachings that Jesus taught us.

You ask why the Church in its totality does not follow this regimen. That question is not for me, or this missive to answer.

This Practice is <u>Not Limited to Catholics</u>, but may be practiced by anyone desiring a close relationship with the Holy Spirit.

<u>What Are Some Of The Unique Practices Of The Charismatic Christians</u>

One of the <u>Unique Practices</u> of the Charismatic Christian which is different for the typical Catholic is, <u>Resting in the Spirit</u>. To the regular, "Cradle Catholic," this practice is strange and raises many questions. Such as, What is Going on? And What is the Purpose of this strange behavior?

When we are Resting in the Spirit we are in a state of full consciousness but have a peace that is totally empty of all thoughts, concerns, or of anything else which would be a diversion from this total peace. If you will, it is <u>Resting in God's Peace</u>, which is a Holy Place.

When we are prayed over to gain this state of Total Peace, we experience a Oneness With God and a Total Peace with the world. It is Wonderful. When passing into this state by prayer, we totally relax and fall limply to the floor. We always have "catchers to prevent injury, but no one has ever been hurt. They just "crumple" to the floor in a totally relaxed state. We can choose how long we desire to be in this state and most usually arise in around 15-minutes.

Another "<u>Unique Practice</u>" is <u>Speaking in Tongues</u>. Most do not understand this practice, and question what is going on.

At the original Pentecost when Jesus's Apostles were gathered in the Upper Chamber with Mother Mary the "Tongues of Fire came down upon them and they <u>Began to Speak in Tongues</u>. All the others were amazed as they heard words in their own language. The words heard by them were words of Praise to God.

Many, if not most of us have been given the gift of <u>Speaking in Tongues</u>. It usually seems to be given to those who become Charismatic Christian. All desire it because it is a method of Praising God. At first, I wondered what the words meant until it was revealed to me that, "God gave me His words of Praise to be repeated back to Him." This satisfied me.

Some rules which seem to be in practice by the Holy Spirit are:

When praying privately to God, the Words are not revealed as God knows what they mean.

When in a group, and one person prays in tongues, there is always an interpreter of the message for the group, and another who confirms the accuracy of the interpretation! This is to benefit the group as the message is a Teaching from God for the Group.

Sometimes, this will be a message for one of those in attendance. Rarely, this may be in their own native language! The interpreter will have this capability.

<u>Why Become A Charismatic Christian?</u>

We want <u>To Live Our Faith to the Fullest, and to Live as Jesus Taught Us.</u>
<u>We Desire to Practice the Gifts of the Holy Spirit.</u>

<u>How Does One Become A Charismatic Christian?</u>

To become a Charismatic Christian requires a process of, ideally, attending a 6-week training Program culminating in a "<u>Hands On</u>" Prayer Session which gives the Holy Spirit to the individual. This may be administered by a Priest, or by those who have been given the Holy Spirit. This is like, if not identical to the Original Apostles being given the Spirit after the 40-days of waiting in the upper Room after Jesus's death. That was when the "Tongues of Fire" came down on them and they began speaking in foreign languages praising God and all of His Works.

This Process is, "Baptism in the Holy Spirit." There is an established, formal process to accomplish this program.

We "<u>Die to Self</u>" and become One with the Holy Spirit; we let Him "<u>Rule Our Lives</u>."

We Practice the Gifts of the Holy Spirit, such as Praying for Healing, Loving Everyone, and Helping Our Neighbor, Just like what Jesus Taught Us.

<u>We Are Unique</u>

It is said there are three types of people. There are those who make things happen, those who watch what happens, and those who wonder, what happened?

That is an oversimplification of the real world because each one of us is unique in our own way. As the Catholic Bishop at my Confirmation ceremony stated it, "You should never be envious of anyone. Of all the people who have been born in the past, all presently living, and all those yet to be created, there is no one like you. You are an unique individual." He went on to say that we must know and use the gifts and talents we have been given.

How are we different? And more importantly, why are we different? Let me count the ways.

<u>How We Become Different</u>

We are created differently from each other. At time of **conception,** when we are created, Our Father in Heaven personally designs each of us and gives each our own gifts, talents, and handicaps. He creates us out of His Love for us, and since true love is only possible if given freely, He gives us the gift of **Free Will.**

Forever after this, He treats each of us as His only Child. To Him, we are unique individuals which He loves beyond measure. He always knows what we are thinking, what we are speaking, and what we are doing. He literally knows every hair on our head and accounts for each of them.

His love for us knows no bounds and is beyond our comprehension to know and understand.

<u>Why Did God Create Us</u>

God created the entire universe, in which we live, for His Own Pleasure. To us, it is vast. To Him, it is the size of a hazelnut in His left palm. That places us in comparison to His Majesty.

He created first the angels to serve him, and to be His companions. Having no will of their own, they could only adore, worship, and serve Him.

As we know from our own experience, we need someone like us to share in our experience of enjoying the beauty of creation. To have companions to share this gift with us is the very substance of Love. God desired this Love for himself. Therefore, **God is Love.**

So, God created all of us, His Children, to share in His Love for His Creation, and in His Love for us. We are truly **All in All** with God and with each other. This is His Gift to us, and to Himself.

God created us in **His Image,** so we are like God in every respect except that He remains in control of us and of all things. We can only gain our position that God has prepared for us by proving that we have total faith and trust in Him and to follow His Will and not our own desires.

When God gave us our own Free Will, there is always the danger that we will follow our desires with the distinct possibility that we could eventually destroy our own home, the earth, which He had prepared for us.

To test for this, and to eliminate our disobedience to Him, He set up a process to control this possibility. This process consists of assigning an entity to operate independently from God with the mission to test all souls to separate from God and to deny Him.

Since Lucifer was the most powerful Angel in Heaven, the most beautiful and the closest to God, he was the obvious choice to accomplish this momentous task. To succeed, the entire scenario must be real and not contrived, or played. It **must be real**!

Lucifer told God that to succeed he required a large contingent to assist him in this enormous task. Lucifer took a third of the angels in heaven to be with him. These are the demons which plague us.

Lucifer, aka Satan, his assigned goal is to wrest us from God's Love and Grace, and carry our souls to hell where they will suffer in fire with Satan. This is to punish those who refuse God's Love and Mercy.

Those of us who develop a personal and intimate relationship with Jesus Christ will never stray, nor drift away from Him. They, we, will always be one with Him.

<u>Adam and Eve – Our Downfall</u>

God knew we would fail our very first test for we were like teenagers without life experience, so we were vulnerable to temptation. This was our first test and we failed miserably. But we would learn by suffering for our disobedience to God. It is said that ninety percent of learning is from making mistakes. That is a heavy price to pay, but most likely, we will remember and be obedient from the experience. With every subsequent test we are presented again with the opportunity to fail. Our lives are filled with temptations, but also with God's appeal to us to come to Him and remain with Him for He is our Savior.

A sidenote: God the Father, consists of three personas, Himself, His Son Jesus, and the Holy Spirit. All are active. God Our Father, who initially designed us, gives us His Spirit at conception which is within us and is our spirit in Him. In this life on earth God desires that we learn Obedience to Him, which is Love for Him. **Love is Obedience to Him**.

And **Love begets Love**. Our destiny is to be with Him in Heaven for all eternity. Therefore, we shall enjoy His Creation with Him, thus fulfilling His Purpose for His creation.

God, Our Father who Created us, is **Always in Control**. He either **Causes** events to happen or **Allows** them to occur for **His Purpose**. Frequently we do not understand why some things are allowed, but as He said in Holy Scripture, "You do not think like I do, and I do not think like you." God sees everything and his purposes are for the ultimate good of all. One aspect that we must acknowledge is that our bodies will die, but our spirit cannot be destroyed; our spirit is immortal. Also, we will not be given more than we can tolerate. God's **Justice** demands some punishment, but His **Mercy** is always present.

We do not Control Anything. We are given Free Will at Conception to choose our actions according to the situations presented to us. If we live with **Devotion to God** in our Heart and Mind, we will be in communication with Him. We shall know when and what He speaks to us. We will recognize His Voice as separate from the voice of Satan.

When I was first called by the Holy Spirit to Jesus, I was hesitant as I had been told that Satan can imitate His voice perfectly. A spiritual friend told me to test the voice by asking the question, "Were you born of the virgin Mary?" The answer would have to be answered truthfully. When I tried this, Jesus response was, "You do not test God." He continued with, "I do not shout." And He finished with the real test, which is, "If the action results in **Good**, then it is from **Me**. If it results in **Evil**, then it is from the **Evil One**."

God Never Changes. He is the Same Now as He has always been. **God is Truth** and will Never Change.

There is only one Absolute. **God's Truth** is the **Only Constant and** never changes. Our God establishes what is **Real** and that is **His Truth**. Living in this world we are given the perception of truth. These perceptions, which are called truth, are forever changing. **Truth never changes. Truth will Endure, everything else will pass away.**

Pursuit Of Truth

"Know the Truth and the Truth will set you free." Attribution unknown.

The better question is, "What is the Purpose of Truth?" Think and meditate on this until you have some knowledge.

Pontius Pilate stated it very succinctly, "What is Truth?"

The ancient Greek, Diogenes, carried a lantern around saying he was searching for the truth.

What is truth? What is YOUR TRUTH? Why should we need to know Truth?

Where Do You Go To Get Your Truth?

We are all inundated with untruths, mistruths, outright lies, knowingly and unknowingly. We are all being programmed to respond and to act as the "powers that be" wish us to act. This is primarily for monetary reasons.

I have begun to utilize a new technique to help in discovering the Truth,

"Follow the Money!"

What Does Webster Say About Truth?

"(1): The body of real things, events, and facts: <u>actuality</u>
(2): The state of being the case:<u> fact</u>
(3): Often capitalized: a transcendent fundamental or <u>spiritual reality</u>."

It continues, but these are the essential elements of their description.

My Personal Definition Of Truth Is The Following:

"<u>Truth Never Changes</u>." If it changes, it was not true originally. We have seen so many things that were generally accepted as true, especially scientific "facts," that we have become very skeptical and careful before we accept anything as "Absolute Truth." I make one exception to this rule, Our Creator cannot speak anything but <u>Absolute Truth</u> as He is the origin of everything. GOD IS TRUTH.

People Disagree With The Meaning Of Truth. Why Is This?

First, we think. and believe, that we are thinking, rational human beings. In my humble opinion (IMHO), we are not; we are emotional creatures, and this is a good thing! This is a very important part of our survival skills. In fact, it is critical. When we are presented with a situation which requires immediate action, there is no time to think it through and to determine the best way to react. We must act, NOW! We automatically shift into our subconscious survival mode and act with instant action, "fight or flight."

There are many ways to see situations. We tend to settle on one "best" solution to problems we encounter; this is OUR solution which we regard as best, this is **Our Truth** for this subject matter.

We are extremely limited in our vision of things. We can only see a very small portion of events due to our position of observation. We are adamant that we saw events as they occurred, but we have a very small window based on our location at the time of the event. We believe we were present, observed, and recorded the event in our memory. So many opportunities for error. Where is Truth? How to be sure?

There is SO MUCH we do not know, and most we will never know. In point of fact, "**We do not know what we do not know!**" therefore, we do not pursue the subject matter to obtain the TRUTH."

Why Do We Need Truth?

"So we can understand what is happening to us?"

Our system of Government is the best that man has been able to develop thus far. Our forefathers who wrote our Constitution were well educated people, and with a real interest in history. I have visited some of their libraries in their homes which have been preserved, and they had all of the historical books of past civilizations. They KNEW what had failed and why prior systems of government had failed.

Their intent was to "invent" a new way of government which avoided all of the problems which had resulted in failures throughout history.

There is one factor which they did not foresee, and could not have envisioned, is the career politician! All of our early leaders just wanted to get the work accomplished of setting up the original government and signing of the agreement, the Constitution, and get back home.

In their wildest dreams they could not imagine anyone in the future wanting to stay in Washington. Otherwise, they would have made term limits part of Our Constitution.

<u>Our Form Of Government</u>

We have the best form of Government that mankind has been able to develop so far. The problem is that it is corrupt, just like every Government that has ever been tried. Inevitably, at some point, Personal Interest and Gain overrides what is good for the people. This is just how we are as human beings. I am not saying that there is not a lot of Good in our Governmental processes, but that there is this factor with which it may be impossible to engineer a system which will prevent personal bias in all circumstances.

I will render a brief scenario of how Our Government works in the real world which we all must live in.

We have a Republic, not a Democracy. This means we have a representative Government where we elect Representatives to go to Congress and who represent our interests in the nation's affairs. This is taught in school.

What is not taught is how this works in actual practice. We elect our Senators and Representatives by choosing and voting for them. To get elected requires money, lots of money which the candidates do not have. So money is raised for each candidate's election. What are the sources of this money. From individual contributions, from large corporations, and from people with special interests who have a special interest in who gets elected. These corporations and special interest groups frequently (usually) give equally to both parties. This ensures their interests are served by whichever candidate gets elected. When a bill comes up for vote in Congress, representatives from these contributors go to the ones who will vote on the bill and tell them how they want them to vote. If they do not follow their request, no more money will be given to get elected; at least that is the implied threat. These people are called lobbyists and are many in Washington, <u>typically three to four for each Senator</u>

and Representative in Congress, **From each special interest group**! Washington is heavily populated by lobbyists.

Now there are a few, very few, who manage to get elected by a "grass roots" effort and do go to Washington to serve their people. However, if they do not join in the "give and take" of the others, they do not get on any committees and cannot have any real influence on legislation before Congress. They usually "get with the program" or serve only one term.

To put it Bluntly, Congress is "Bought and Paid For" as far as the general public is concerned. To protect our own interests we must, organize a large group of people, which will provide a single voice, and hire our own Lobbyist. Of course, this is only one lobbyist against an army of opposing forces, but I have seen the effectiveness of this one lobbyist when they have **Truth** on their side.

Where Do You Get Your Truth?

We get our information from the media of course, and from the internet. Also, from personal experience and hearsay. We have already discussed the opportunities for error in personal observation, and of course we are only too aware of the obvious biases of the media, political, financial, and commercial interests always drive the policies of the media organizations. Let us never forget this! The point is, the entire world is driven by **Money, Not Truth**!

I find the quickest way to the Truth is to Follow the Money. Money doesn't just Talk, it always reveals the Truth.

I use a technique which I learned from working in Quality Organizations where we established defect patterns which lead to the "root cause" of the defect. When we could identify the True Cause of the defect, we could eliminate it from the overall process.

This technique is very simple and can be applied everywhere and to anything. Ask Why, Why, Why until there are no more Whys to be answered. We have arrived at the Truth! It is in this discovery process that we encounter the problems of evasion, protection of self-interest, huge efforts of protection of personal egos, and many other obstructions. I have never posited that the production of the Real Truth, which is real and never changes, is TRIVIAL or EASY.

Life is a process. It is a continuum of events with no discontinuities. Each event is directly connected to the next event," One thing leads to another." It is very predictable.

When Truth is exposed, things CHANGE! Usually, big changes happen. When we live by truth alone, life is completely different. Jesus taught us that fact. It got Him killed because we base our lives on self-interest, which is usually at the expense of our fellow "brothers and sisters." Truth dispels the "Game of Life," and the "Well Laid Plans of Mice and Men." Man's plans to control their own destiny at the expense of others, cannot survive Truth!

<u>Truth Is Critical In Life</u>

If we learn our lessons in life using erroneous information, we develop wrong conclusions and make bad decisions, for ourselves, and for our world.

Life is a process, just like everything that occurs. If we input to, and use wrong information in this process, we will have unacceptable results. We find our world in this state at present.

People Love to hear the Truth. They know it when they hear it!

I encourage all of you to stop, sit in a quiet place with no interruptions, and spend some time with nothing else on your mind, and THINK! Meditate if you will. Think as you have never thought before. Think for yourself, and in your mind observe what will be the results of the conclusions you reach. You are free to your own ideas about what is Right and Wrong, what is Acceptable, and more importantly, what is Not Acceptable! Take Full Responsibility for your own Actions and those of your leaders. Remember, they represent your desires and beliefs.

It is amazing what surfaces from this exercise in discovering the Real Truth. Nothing less will make any sense to you, and you will reject many things when you put it to this test.

What Is A Man And What Is A Woman

God measured and designed **Woman** similar to **Man**. He did **Not make Her identical to Man.**

God has a Plan for each of us that is Distinct and Unique. There is No Room for Changes. God gave us Free Will, but this is to be restricted within the Confines of His Plan. When we deviate, we are risking separation from Him.

We may think, wish, and desire to choose our own path, but it is risky to oppose God. God Made Man, and Woman, and we are His.

Man Is different from Woman; both have unique and special characteristics. This is for their **Roles** that God has planned for them.

Whoever changes their sexual role, is placing themselves in God's Wrath.

Some Key Characteristics of a Man? - In No Special Order

Honest	Reserved	Responsible
Confident	Humble	Spiritual
Reverent	Patient	Respectful
Truthful	Protective	

Some key Characteristics of Women

Warm	Nurturing	Caring
Loving	Giving	Unselfish
Creative	And Many More	

What Is A Woman

God measured and designed **Woman** similar to **Man.** He did **Not make Her identical to Man.**

God has a Plan for each of us that is Distinct and Unique. There is No Room for Changes. God gave us Free Will, but this is to be restricted within the confines of His Plan. When we deviate, we are risking separation from Him.

We may think, wish, and desire to choose our own path, but it is risky to oppose God. God Made Man, and Woman, and we are His.

MARRIAGE AND DIVORCE

Why do we divorce? Because we, ourselves, come before all others. Our needs, our desires, and our very being, always come first, and if the partner does not meet and mesh with this, then we must have a change in partners. It is termed, "A Deal Breaker."

We feel we must be happy and we look to our partner to make this come true for us. We do know no one is happy all the time, but if our lack of satisfaction is too pervasive, we must make a change.

Why do we not deal with this possibility before marriage? We do not! We are, "In Love!"

When I was young, I asked my mother, "How will I know I am in love?" My mother replied, "You will know." I asked again, "How will I know?"

Again, she said, "You will just know." I said, "But how will I know?" Then she said, "You will want to be with her all of the time!" This is the answer for the test of true love. After 65-years of marriage I still felt this way! I never had this desire to be with another.

I have the opportunity, from time to time, to consult with young men just before their marriage. I ask them, "What are you going to give up?" They reply with surprise, "What do you mean?" I tell them that since we all have only 24 hours in a day, and 7-days a week, when we get married and enter into a close partnership with another, we have to make time for them, to share in mutual pursuits and just to be together since that is the culmination of being in love with another. They are astounded since they have never thought of this. Their only consideration has been to add these activities to their current interests.

The failure to spend quality time with our loved ones is one of the primary causes of failed marriages. This must be in our plans before marriage!

One of the sure signs that our partner is compatible is we talk and talk, and just want to be with them and talk some more. We just enjoy being with them and do not want to be apart. Sharing interests is a positive, but is not required. After my 65-years of marriage to my wife, I still want to be with her instead of being anywhere else.

This sounds so ideal, and it is. Everyone does not have this happen to them. It is a gift from God, and we must allow Him to give it to us. I have learned, over my lifespan, that we must allow things to come to us, we cannot force them to happen. A hard lesson, but necessary, since we do not have the power to change anything, or anyone, besides ourselves. Even changing our own attitude and behavior is usually extremely difficult, and usually painful. I have learned that if we just, "Let Go, and Let God conduct our lives, all good will come to us. It is so easy when we apply this to our daily lives. But, we are all "Control Freaks," and it is so hard to let go of all our plans and yes, schemes at times, and just, "Go with the Flow of Life."

I have heard it said that "Marriage is a 50-50 proposition. It is not! It is a 100-100 percent relationship. Each person must be prepared, and willing, and ready to give up all of themselves to the other person in the relationship if it is to endure. If it is truly love, in your eyes and God's eyes, you will have this desire in your heart.

In Marriage - You Are Right

With my marriage to my wife of 65-years, we bickered for many years. We called ourselves, "The Bickersons." Most times, we could not remember what the argument was about. My wife used to record them in an attempt to try to understand the cause of the disagreement.

That is, until it came to me, from the Holy Spirit I am sure, that always being right was not a good objective. It causes disruption in families, hard feelings, and creates distances between those who should be lovers!

In the long view, it is disastrous. It can result in breakups and divorce. In the grand scheme of things, **it is not important to be right!**

Realizing this, I immediately started telling my wife, "You are right!" even at those times I was totally certain I had the right answer, and she did not. Who cares?

After a short while of my practicing this new technique, my wife picked up on what was happening and began to use this same technique herself! This ended our arguments, fights, and failures to communicate.

This is a Miracle in itself!

Sexual Component In God's Love

There is a sexual component in God's Love for us, His Children.

In marriage we become one with each other. In our **Union with God**, we become One with Him.

Relations between husband and wife is the ultimate expression of God's love and our love for each other.

Out of this Union comes Life in Abundance.

A SERIES OF MIRACLES

INTRODUCTION

This is my story of personal witness to miracles written at the suggestion of my Priest, Father Nicholas Wichert at St. Brendan's Catholic Church in Bothell, Washington state. This was after I related to him that my entire life has been a series of miracles. He told me I should write it in a book.

I write this as a report of my experience of miracles for two reasons:

For witness to the goodness of God for us all.

1. To encourage everyone to look for, in their own lives, the miracles that are given to us.

I believe that we all have the Power of God in the form of The Holy Spirit guiding us constantly, and we can benefit greatly if we recognize this and allow God to lead us in our lives.

The impetus for writing this book is an experience which I had several years ago. I was asked to do a "Personal Witness" before a group from a sister Parish who was exploring areas which our church had been involved in for several years. My personal witness had nothing to do with the subject matter to be discussed, but was to begin the meeting. I had no idea what to say, but the Holy Spirit provided the subject matter and the words.

I began with, "My birth mother died when I was three years old, and my dad passed away when I was fourteen." I went on to describe briefly what happened during these periods of my life. I was told after my talk that I had all of the women crying. Next I repeated my talk, but this time I included all of the positives which followed each of these events.

My Life Story of Miracles Begins

Frederick Garland Mackaman - Born October 7, 1932

My birth mother died of pneumonia and childbirth when I was three years old.

My dad, at 44-years old, married a 19-years old girl/woman to take care of me. She told me years later she married him just so she could raise me. From the first time we met in a restaurant when I wouldn't eat, she got me to eat. I called her, "muvver." This was my new mother that God sent for me. **A miracle!**

A major **miracle,** and a very major turning point in my life.

My new mother's family were devoted Assembly of God Church people and were very humble, and spiritual in everything they did. For every major decision, they would meet as a family group and pray over the decision seeking the answer.

However, my new mother was a rebel and was not into that at all. She gave me all her love.

My Early Life

- My Life in the Army - 1953-1955 Always pushed ahead in leadership roles. Many **Miracles**.
- My Finding My Soul Mate and Companion
- My Work Career
- My Drinking Problem - Began with business trips, continued after that. Finally, one day, that just stopped! I didn't even notice I wasn't drinking that night. No desire. Major, major **Miracle.**
- Three years and two months before God's Call and baptism, is when I stopped drinking; my mind expanded tremendously as I was given the gift of understanding and suddenly, I could understand things I could never understand before. My hair had turned gray, and I was physically going downhill fast since retirement. Now this entire process was dramatically reversed, and I looked much younger. Even now, at 90-years of age, people cannot believe my age. I look like I am in my 50's! My mind is in my 30's.
- On Mother's Day, 2005, I had this life changing epiphany, which was called by God. A major **Miracle, a once in a lifetime experience.**
- Baptized September 26, 2005 Confirmed February 10, 2006.

I became a Charismatic soon after baptism. I have had deep spiritual experiences in Boca Raton and Bothell Catholic Churches.

God talks to me frequently, guiding me in what He wants me to do for Him and for His children.

My Life In The Army

I was called into the U. S. Army, and served during the Korean War at Ft. Lewis, Washington for 2-years. My mother prayed for me since all the basic training groups preceding mine, were sent directly to the front lines. My cycle of training was the first to not be sent directly there; we were disbursed to several different places. My mother considered this a **Miracle** and an answer to her prayer. Since I had applied for and been accepted as a candidate for Officers Candidate School (OCS), I was placed in the Division Replacement Company to await orders.

I experienced several **Miracles** during my tour of duty. In basic training all the squad leaders were replaced after the first 8-weeks of training. I was one of those appointed to replace those who were removed and to become a squad leader, which consisted of being responsible for eleven other individual soldiers in my squad. This was my first leadership role. I had all leadership positions after this. I consider this a minor **Miracle.**

I applied for Officer Candidate School (OCS) and was accepted to attend Artillery OCS which is the one I had selected, and I awaited orders until the next class was to begin.

While I was awaiting orders, the Army Base Division established a program to improve community relations with the local population. A competition was held to select the "Soldier of the Week." This was out of the entire division population of approximately thirty-five thousand soldiers. Much to my shock, and surprise, I was selected. This was indeed a major **Miracle.** Included in the planned rewards for this was an evening on the town of Tacoma, a new Pontiac to use, a date with the town beauty queen, tickets to a major show, and dinner at the best steak house. I also could bring a buddy and we had accommodation at the best hotel in town for the night.

As Soldier of the Week, I spent a week with the Post Commander, a One-Star General, and a week with the Division Commander, a Two-Star General. This General told me that every Division Commander had the prerogative of appointing two candidates to West Point each year. He offered me one of those positions! This was a rare opportunity for the competition for entry to West Point is tremendous. A special opportunity. A real **Miracle!** I politely declined the offer. I had already determined that the Army was not the life for me. I have always valued creativity and having tried it twice during my service interval, I found it to be totally unacceptable, to put it mildly. Taking orders exactly is the only mode that would be tolerated.

At a future point in my life, I was hired by IBM, another **Miracle** for me, and they rewarded creativity!

A Very Unusual Miracle

The Healing of an item of furniture:

Recently I was opening packages while sitting in my programmable recliner chair. I knew that I shouldn't be opening boxes with my pocketknife while sitting there. I always opened boxes at the kitchen counter in case my knife slipped and went beyond the box edge.

My knife slipped and slit the top of the left arm of my chair for a length of about one-half inch. I was devastated! I could not repair this, and it was in a most conspicuous location. I could not come up with an answer to solve this problem. Duct tape was totally out of the question. This is a very expensive, state-of-the-art chair and it would have to be completely re-upholstered, which was not really feasible as it also had a special material which even the cats' scratching couldn't damage. I could not come up with any solution to this problem which I had caused.

I decided to just do nothing for the present until I could come up with an acceptable answer to my huge problem.

God, The Holy Spirit, had other plans.

Out of nowhere, a tape like substance was placed over the tear. It was translucent, and was slightly wider, and longer than the tear. I just watched it over the next four or five days. Slowly, day by day, the tape and tear got smaller. At the end of this period, the cut area was **entirely gone!**

A major, major Miracle! Unheard of for this type of healing of an inanimate object.

Our Destiny Depends Upon Us

Our God Created Us and gave us Free Will. He did this so we could gain the Power to Choose Him; to Choose Him In Love, and

For Love! With this Power we were given other Powers, the Power to Control Our Destiny!

After God Creates each of us, His Children, He follows each of us Perfectly and treats each as An Only Child!

God Awaits and Observes what each of us do with our Thoughts, Words, and Actions. This is the Determinant of the Future!

What Actions We Take has an Effect, and All Actions by Everyone Taken Together, Changes World Events!

God can influence Our Thoughts, and Hearts, but we Take the Actions.

For True Love for God to be Real, and Effective, it must be Given Freely!

So, the Future is Determined by Our Actions, not Predetermined by God. However, He can alter time to accommodate His agenda. He can shorten and extend intervals of time at His Will. We do not recognize these changes. With God, everything must be orderly and in follow in sequence.

Let us be Entirely Clear; God is Always in Charge of Everything! He makes some Good from every Evil. Yet God allows us the Freedom to Choose Good from Evil. Our Time on Earth is a Testing Time, and the Time and Events are determined by our Actions. This is a Learning Process for us, His Children.

God's Plan is that All Be Saved. We all suffer during this Process. Some suffer more, and others may suffer less; this is all for God to Decide. If there are Some who will not Repent and Accept God, then He Promised Eternal Suffering in Hell.

God is a God of Mercy which makes it extremely difficult for me to even imagine Him accepting even one of his Children, whom He Personally Created and Loves, to be lost for all Eternity! Our God will find a way to Incent the Unsaved to Come to Him. That is My Hope and My Prayer!

Padre Pio's Affect On Me

One day our charismatic leader suggested we go to mass at a sister church that day. It was in the afternoon at the same time as our usual charismatic meeting at our Catholic Church. Perhaps it was arranged.

At that mass and after it was over, I had an opportunity to pray over a pair of Padre Pio's gloves. These were under glass for protection. I had read about Padre Pio and some of his exploits and manifestations. He was known for his ability to "bio-locate." He was ordered by his bishop to remain in his station in the church, yet he was verified to be in another city at the same time conducting confessions. This was verified by church authorities. He was well known for the effectiveness of his confessions received from others who came to him.

What he was most noted for was his bleeding from the "Wounds of Christ." He suffered for years from this, up to the day of his death.

At some point in my life with Christ, He asked me, "Would you take on my Wounds?" I was astounded by this and had no immediate reply! I knew of all the difficulties suffered by Padre Pio and could not imagine how I could deal with that. I did not answer; I cogitated for weeks. Finally, immediately after taking on His Body and Blood during mass, the top of my right hand began to swell up with blood. The skin did not break so there was no external bleeding. I knew that God was using this device to assist me in making this decision. It took me two weeks to dwell on this until I finally could answer God. I told Him, "Lord, I just cannot deal with this." At this time, I did not know that there are several in the world who have responded positively to God's request to take on His Wounds. For example, some only bleed on Thursdays.

This was the second biggest mistake, and regret of my life in denying God's request!

The first was when He spoke to me directly for the first time. Before He brought me into His Church, I was looking in the mirror at myself and He spoke to me, "If you stop drinking now, it will not affect your memory." Did I stop, no; could I stop, I don't know. I just ignored the entire incident. **Never ignore God, and never refuse His requests.**

I suffered for forty long years after that until He rescued me one night. I stopped drinking, and He gave me All His Gifts of Knowledge, Wisdom, and Power, the Gifts of the Holy Spirit. My mind was expanded to understand things that I had never been able to understand. I had been getting gray and losing my physical abilities. My wife had told me, "You will be dead in 6-months." My hair went back to its original color, my strength was restored, my mind was created anew!

All this occurred 3-years and 2-months **Before** he brought me into His Church!

ADDENDUM:

Life Is The Answer

Life is the answer to Life. Allow me to explain.

Many people search for the meaning of life; why are we here, what is our purpose? The answers to these questions are very simple.

We are here to Love and Serve God, Our Creator, and to Love and Serve our neighbor, who are all of our brothers and sisters in this world.

These are the two most important Commandments in the Bible, as stated by Jesus in answer to the question.

Why is this true? We struggle and strive for personal happiness, and it seems all we do is go from one problem to the next. We enjoy no long-lasting satisfaction. We suffer and wonder why we go through such misery while doing our very best to do the right thing.

The truth is we do not derive our rewards and satisfactions by doing for ourselves, but by doing for others. When we work for our own personal happiness, we are on the path to selfishness, which has no lasting reward. In fact, it is considered a sin in God's Eyes. When we do for others as our main goal in life, we derive the highest level of joy in spite of sometimes suffering hardships in the process. We all suffer in this life; there is no escape from this truth, but it is certainly possible to suffer and experience joy at the same time. This appears to be impossible, yet it is true as many will attest.

When we travel this road, we will be on the highway to experience joy in this life and eternal happiness in the Life to Come with God.

<u>Our Human Nature</u>

Human Nature is self-serving. Why is this? From Adam and Eve, we all are born self-serving. We are like the demanding baby, the spoiled teenager, and the adult who always considers themselves first. Even when we think we are being equal with others, we always make certain our needs and desires are met first. That is our inborn nature.

Psychological studies have shown that we always give ourselves a ten percent edge in order to be sure we are served. Actual life experience with this principle of, **Separate But Equal**, has proven this is the case. We try to be entirely fair with the distribution of goods between races. The other race gets their share after we take our pick of the best.

In my humble view, it is the basic principle of, "If it for myself, it is the essence of evil and is one of the prime drivers of evil in our nature. If we are driven by the altruistic goal of you first, then my share, this is Holy and from the Holy Spirit which is God."

This is part of His testing our Free Will for conformity to His Will, which is, "All Good for All His Children." We choose for ourselves first, then we suffer from the problems this causes, then we learn and grow in God's Grace and advance in our quest for Heaven.

As we travel in this life to follow God's Plan for us, we first climb out of the sludge of the pit, get on the bridge, then begin the long, arduous journey up the mountain to our goal of gaining the peak where we are to encounter Our God. While we are on this journey, we are to help others over huge boulders, deep pits, ridges, and barriers which are vast impediments in our progress to Heaven. This is the message given to Saint Elizabeth of Sienna in her biography. Every Catholic should read this book as it contains direct answers from God to her questions for our salvation.

<u>Understanding Unbelievers</u>

I have always had a great deal of difficulty understanding why some people cannot accept God's Word.

For me, it is so simple and fundamental. God cannot tell a lie, and by definition, His Word is True!

Most people probably accept this Truth; so why cannot they act on His Message to us? It is all a mystery to me; it seems so simple.

Another thing with unbelievers, especially atheists, "If they have not seen it, touched it, or tasted it or smelled it, or experienced it in some manner, it does not exist!" If they, personally, have not determined it exists, then they refuse to accept the new reality no matter the authority.

There is one caveat to this. If the new information supports their own agenda, then they accept it as real.

What we have not experienced with God, we cannot imagine! To appreciate God and what He offers to us, His children, we must have our own Personal Experience With Him.

<u>You Become What You Think About</u>

You are what you think about. If you consciously decide on what you think about for most of your time, you are very unusual!

If you let random thoughts create the content of your mind, you are like normal people.

However, when you allow a serious subject to enter your mind, you probably become more disciplined in your approach.

How you spend your time in your mind is important; it determines who you are! The old saying, "Pick your friends carefully, as you will become just like them," applies here also.

This Key Life Principle is the prime reason people are different.

My Proclamation - God's Word

"I have called you, and I await your response. Come to me as I have conceived you in Love, for Love, and to Love as I have Loved you.

Your Purpose is to be with Me Forever in Heaven to Share in My Love for My Creation. You are My Children whom I Love Perfectly, and desire for you to be with me forever.

I Love You, and you love Me. This is your purpose. Come and Join Me. Do not delay your acceptance of My Offer of Mercy. I Desire for you to be with Me.

Those who dawdle and delay are risking the punishment I have planned for those who do not accept Me Readily. All will come to Me; some after great suffering.

Be grateful and come to Me Now!"

The Power Of Self

We possess all that Jesus has in God the Father's Spirit. We are given this at conception. He gives us all that we are, which is identical to Him.

He is our King and we are obedient to His Spirit. We have the capability to love Him, and all our brothers and sisters in Christ with unlimited devotion.

We are given the Power of Christ to Love Him with All Our Heart, with All Our Soul, with All Our Spirit, with All Our Mind, and with All Our Strength. To fully realize this Power, we must Surrender our own Will to Him so we may be One With Him and enjoy all the Father of the Spirit has given us!

The Lord's Plan

- God is Good, He is Perfect in Goodness
- God allows Trials to Test Us
- He helps us in Our Trials, especially if we ask Him
- We Suffer in these Trials as we All Suffer Trials in this Life

- He will never give Us anything beyond our capacity to endure
- Those who Persevere will Advance to Heaven
- There is no more Testing or Trials in Heaven
- Only Those who Have Endured will Be in Heaven
- We Will All Be Perfect in Heaven as God is Perfect

Everything Happens For A Purpose

God has a purpose and Plan for everything! He has the power to alter His Plan at any time and for His Reasons.

We are to Obey His Plans as He makes them known to us! Obedience is how we display our love for him!

God is always in charge! He either causes events to occur, or allows them for His Purposes. We do not, nor can we understand His reasons; that is not our purpose. Our mission is to obey Him.

Satan was allowed to be the Prince of this world at the time of Adam and Eve, and used by God to test us for our obedience. We learn, and grow from our mistakes.

God's Goal is for all of His Children whom He Created, to know Him, seek Him, and devote themselves entirely to Love of Him.

There will be a Time for Reconciliation with God; we must be prepared for this at all times.

When Jesus Returns, He will return in Glory and will assume Control of this world. The faithful will be justified!

Journey To Innermost God

The journey to Our God leads us to where He resides, in the innermost location in our soul.

God provides a path for us to reach Him as we progress along the journey to that goal.

This process is at the discretion of Our God, and to how arduously we pursue Him. The decision is ours to fulfill.

The are many steps along the way and many difficulties to be overcome. God is in charge, but our progress is dependent upon our desire and how arduously we pursue Him. God provides the way and Satan provides the temptations to impede us and slow our progress.

When we do reach Our Innermost God, we will have achieved our Oneness with Him, and will forevermore be With Him and be All in All with All of His Elect.

Total Surrender To God

Belief and Faith cannot be explained; they can only be experienced by the giving up of Ones Self's Will and **Surrendering it to God**!

Do not be Confused. "**There is Only One God!**" There are many who are proclaimed, but there is only One Creator of All.

I Am He, who is above everything and the Creator of All!

There is **Only One Truth**! That is God's Truth, since He was The Creator of Everything that was Created.

Anything else comes from the Deceiver, the father of all lies, Satan who seeks to destroy what God has created.

Let us always remember, **Nothing Happens Unless God Creates It, or Allows It To Occur!** He is in **Control of Everything, Always!**

God causes some good to come out of all evil, and **He** allows evil to exist to test our response, and actions from our gift of Free Will. We determine events by our actions; **He** allows this and responds with **His Purpose!**

To Gain Access To The Lord

Spend Time With Him!

- Spend Quiet Time, Just You and Him, Alone Together
- Meditation and Prayer, Not Requests, Just Praise and Worship
- Pray the Rosary, Preferably the Entire Rosary, All 20-Decades
- Adoration, an Hour with Him, either Exposed or in the Tabernacle

God is with us, Constantly!
He knows our every Thought!

We are His Creation, we Belong to Him!

To Become Close to Our God, We must Sacrifice Our Whole Heart and Soul to Him, and to Him Alone! He must become Our Only Priority!

<u>God Is The Only True Reality</u>

God is the Only True Reality! We live by Truth Alone, and the Truth will Set you Free!

We Live In:

<u>An Ever Changing World,</u> Not in Reality!

<u>Nothing Is Real,</u> Everything is Constantly Changing, except for God's Truth, which never changes!

What is Your Truth? Where do you obtain Your Truth. Truth does not change; that is the definition of Truth.

We live by what we believe, what we know, and by what we think we know. We Base All of Our Decisions on these Factors! No wonder we must keep modifying our plans because their basis is constantly changing. Try this to illustrate: Write down your plans for tomorrow, the next week, the next month, and track to see what must change to carry out your plans.

We live in a constantly changing world based upon our own faulty assumptions because we do not have access to the Truth! In my humble experience, almost all Assumptions are False, and do not prove out!

So, what should we do? <u>Depend on God!</u> Back off and <u>"Let Go."</u> "Let God Be God!" How do we do this?

First, we Must Believe in Him, in Everything! -There is <u>Nothing He will Not Forgive!</u>

Open Your Heart and Mind and be <u>Completely Open To Him</u>!

<u>Listen to Him,</u> He will answer you! Do not fill your mind with your thoughts, Let Go and Wait on Him.

Our God is in Control of Everything! <u>Trust in Him Explicitly!</u>

He Can Do <u>Anything, and Everything!</u>

<u>God Makes All the Rules</u> and can Change Them for His Purposes.

Let us <u>Not Limit Our God</u> with our small, worldly thinking.

God Is Always The Same

Our Lord is the Same Now as He Has Always Been! He Never Changes.

He can do whatever He wants in Miracles and in Changing His Laws which He Established!

Our God is Always in Charge of <u>Everything</u>! He either Makes Each Event Occur, or Allows it to Occur, for His Purposes!

God is not Limited by the physical laws of this universe which He established by His Creation. He can change them at any time He wishes for HIs Purposes, so let us not try to limit Him in our thinking and projection of what we expect Our God to accomplish. God has No Limits!

God creates Time for our benefit. He has no need for time as it is only a relational idea which refers to the movement of our planet, earth, in our solar system. He focusses on events and their relation to sequence of events. To gain perspective, this Universe is like a hazelnut in His Left Palm!

There is only <u>One Source for All Original Ideas</u>! That source is God, Our Creator, only He can Create! We are given these ideas to use in the development of everything we do. He allows us to manipulate these ideas and apply the results to accomplish what we wish to make happen.

Satan uses this same technique to manipulate these Original Ideas to accomplish the evil ideas he promotes within us.

There are only two sources for ideas in our conscious mind. God and Satan. We take these inputs and use them to develop our own thinking.

We are all Control Freaks! We want to know everything so we can control our destiny. Only God knows everything!

Our Love of God is what He Desires. We Love Him by Obedience to Him!

We live in this World which is not Reality, it is All Perception, our perception, not what is Truth, which is the True Reality. This world changes constantly; Truth never changes.

The definition of Truth is, "Truth Never Changes." It always remains the same and is repeatable. God's Word states the Constant, Real Truth.

God's Word Defined

It is so simple! God is Love and the Source of All Truth.
God created all of us in His Love, For Love, so we can Love Him.
God desired Our Love for Him so He created us for that purpose.

For Love to be True Love, it must be given Freely so God gave us Free Will so we can Freely Choose to Love Him. Only this is True Love.

The reason God wanted us to Love Him Freely was so we can share in His Joy with His Creation, and in everything He does.

We are truly One With God. At inception God gave each of us His Spirit so we are all One With God, but He requires that we Choose Him Freely so our love is authentic.

The risk to God is if we do not choose Him, what will result? It could lead to disaster. Even though we have His Spirit and we are created in His Image and with His Spirit, this is new territory for him to explore. God created His Angels to Adore Him, but they do not choose freely. God wanted subjects who could directly share in His Divinity and experience the Joy with His Creations. We are them. Let us Rejoice and participate. Let there be no more reluctance.

To ensure that this experience would always result in Good, God established a Test Plan. Lucifer, being the Best and Highest Angel was chosen to be God's Test Vehicle. Satan, Lucifer, wa given the charge to do his best to test God's Plan to the worst case limits. He is doing exceptionally well.

God's Grace For Us His Children

There is only one way to write about God, and that is with the **Truth.** Many do not want to hear Truth as it does not coincide with the beliefs which they have adopted for themselves. Why is this, we wonder? We humans look for, and accept those things which are easy, fun, pleasurable, and are immediate in results.

Another trait we have is, we are **Control Freaks**. We want to control everything which can affect our lives. We want to be, "In Charge." Therefore, we will only accept, and believe in factors which fit these criteria, or that can be forced into this paradigm.

Truth never will fit this concept; therefore, we continuously live a life filled with events which confound us, and we are constantly in a state of, "Out of Control."

We do not have, and never will have, total control of our lives. Nothing happens unless **God Causes It or Allows it to Occur**. We cause our Own Problems by following our False Beliefs, but God can, and does make Good out of all things.

"There is a reason for Everything." Nothing occurs without the knowledge and involvement of God, the Holy Spirit.

God's Gifts To Us - Our Prayers To Him

As Our Good Father, God freely presents Good Gifts to us. He wants to please us, and it is His Love for us that prompts Him to do this.

However, when we Ask for these gifts, and He responds by granting them, He risks spoiling us by teaching us that He will grant everything we request of Him. This also places us in the position of assuming we can control God's Actions; of course, we cannot do this.

God knows what is in our hearts and what we secretly desire. He also knows what we need, and what is not good for us. He prefers to grant His Gifts to us as He Determines the when and how of this process, and even if our desire should be granted.

One alternative is to Pray, "Father, Thy Will Be Done." However, He does enjoy hearing our prayers, and the communications with us.

When we Pray to Our God, we must take these essential elements into consideration. Every connection we have with Our God is Precious to Him and should be with us.

For Love Of God

There are three parts to the Person of God. These are, God the Father, Jesus, His Only Son, and the Holy Spirit.

In the Church that Jesus founded to teach the principles that God the Father mandated, the Holy Catholic Church, we find that God the Father and Jesus, His Only Son, are revered and covered in the Church's teachings quite thoroughly. The Holy Spirit is only covered in passing and is not emphasized although that is where the Power resides.

We ask, "Why is this?" That is an excellent question, and one which requires investigation. The Charismatic Movement within the Catholic Church concentrates in this factor. Charismatics are little known, and not understand with their practices of, "Tongues, and Resting in the Spirit" even though these are discussed in the Holy Bible.

One day while I was kneeling directly in front of the Tabernacle, I asked God, "How can I love you more?" He responded immediately with, "Be more Holy." I asked, "How can I do this O Lord?" His response was, "Be more Obedient!" So, there it is, For Love of God, be Obedient to His every command, directive, and desire! God Is Love, and to show our Love is to be Obedient to him.

God will either ask you to accomplish a task for him, or He will Tell you to do it. When He tells you, it is a mandatory directive not to be ignored, or put aside. When He Asks you, it is your option with your Free Will to decide. However, He does desire that you follow His Desire, and you put it aside at your own risk.

God doesn't make errors and all His work is Correct. Also, He does not say anything that is not true. He is Perfect!

<u>Let Go And Let God</u>

It has been revealed to me that when we "Let and Let God" take over, miracles can happen. Also, and this is important, we can experience events that normally happen only in Heaven.

Such as, being in one place and transferring to another at merely the thought of it. This is recorded in the Holy Bible in at least two places. When Jesus and the Apostles were in the boat, and the wind had just been calmed by Jesus, they were immediately transported to their destination.

Another instance was when the King's Treasurer had just been instructed as to what the Holy Readings meant, God's Instructor, which He sent to perform this task, was taken to his destination.

My experience is in time. Place is just another manifestation of time. When I pray my Rosary and concentrate on each meaning of each stanza, I frequently am taken from the beginning of the decade to the last part. Some may argue that this is just my mind playing tricks on me, but this must be experienced to believe it.

Think of the experience of having a remote person take over your computer, cursor and all, when you allow this so a problem can be corrected by the expert. This is the same experience as letting God take over our life temporally to solve our problem, hence, a miracle.

The key to allowing this to occur is we must "Let Go and Let God," We must totally let go of all of our thoughts, feelings, and desire to retain control of ourselves! Otherwise, God cannot take over to satisfy our need. He is dependent on us to "Allow" His Control to affect the result.

This principle is in effect when we totally have no control of the result, and "Give Up." Then we are fully open to God's Grace to help us in our distress. This is what He requires to aid us, that we open ourselves to Totally Depend Upon Him.

Amen.

God is Magnificent!

<u>Prayer To God</u>

There are so many ways to communicate with God.

I will list a few here:

Pray using Words. God already knows what is in your heart and what you need. Still, He likes to hear you ask for whatever you need or want. You can also just pray that His Will be done, but always thank Him and Praise His for what He has done and is doing for you.

Praying with the Rosary is a form of Prayer. Pray while concentrating on the meaning of each word. Take care that you do not have another agenda in your thoughts while you are praying this sacred

Rosary. Mother Mary gave the Rosary to us as a gift as her precious way to move us closer to Our God.

Pray without Words! Give God a chance to talk instead of bombarding Him with your words of requests.

Silence is a form of Prayer. You Will receive Knowledge, frequently it is enormous Wisdom that cannot be gained in any other way!

God loves His Children so much that He wants to hear from us, personally, every day. Let us join Him in Prayer.

God Is Infinite

God invented the concept of time for man's convenience and understanding of events. Only distance is a factor of place.

God does not need time for His Uses since He is everywhere at once and sees all things.

Einstein entered the field of mathematics to prove there is a God. He ended by proving in his known mathematical formula of C=MC squared. That is, the limit of speed is mass times the speed of light squared.

If he would have equated that the concept of time is not a factor, he would have entered into his formula the substitution of "0" for the time factor in the speed of light. That is, C=MC squared breaks down to C=mass X 186,000. miles/second. If we replace the factor, "second", with the factor, "0", the entire equation goes to infinity!

So that is where God is, in Infinity, that is <u>God has No Limits</u>.

Who Is A Christian

Everyone who believes in Christ is a Christian, by definition. Christ Jesus is the Son of God, Our Creator.

"Whoever believes in Me will have everlasting life." Paraphrase of, "For God so loved the world, that He gave His only begotten Son, that whosoever believeth in Him should not perish, but have everlasting life." John 3:16 This is the cornerstone belief of the Christian.

God Created everyone to Love Him, and to Love Each Other. Why do we not believe this, and why is this not happening? It seems we have this innate desire to serve ourselves first, and if anything of our love happens to be left over, we can use this to serve others, and perhaps God; that is, if we even recognize Him.

What a selfish attitude! It seems we are selfish creatures, by nature. Why is this you ask? Now this leads to a long story; in fact, this is the story of the Bible. You can read all about it there; over and over this story is repeated.

There are those who Do Believe in Christ Jesus. How, and why are they different, you ask? Where do they get this idea that God is real and is in Jesus? Many have discovered for themselves that God, who is Our Father and Creator, His Son Jesus, and the Holy Spirit, presumably Their Spirit, are All One Together, just One Person!

A Lesson which I have learned, or better yet, have been taught by God, is this: A Belief System, or Religion if you prefer, cannot be taught for understanding by others, it must be Experienced! Only then can it be Accepted as Real and Personal. Frequently, it is simply a Gift from God. However, we must be open to God to receive it. <u>A Gift cannot be given</u> <u>unless there is a desire to receive it!</u>

<u>Accessing The Inner Self</u>

The process of accessing the Inner Self has not been understood. Many have pursued this goal for thousands of years.

It can be explained on several levels, 1) Physical, 2) Psychological, 3) Mental, 4) Spiritual, and there may be other ways.

I choose the Spiritual Way since I am more familiar with this as I am what is called, a "Charismatic Christian." What is this? It is striving to live according to the Way that Jesus instructed us to live. You may ask, how is this different than the traditional way that is taught by existing Christian Religions? The answer to that question is very simple; we attempt to live this Way to the very best of our ability, even though we cannot be perfect as Jesus was. We do not "Cherry Pick" what we choose to believe in; we take His Teachings seriously and follow them exactly as taught with no changes, additions, or deletions!

To get into the state of Oneness with your Spirit can be achieved in several ways. I choose to explain the way I am most familiar with.

Place yourself in a state of quiet, and alone from all distractions.

Relax → "Let Go" → Release of All thoughts and feelings → Become Totally Open to God (Who is Always within Us.) → Totally Surender to Him - Retain Nothing For Yourself → Giving Up All Control of Self – Only Open to God Himself.

You will feel nothing but perhaps Euphoria, or just Perfect Peace and **At One With the Word**. You will be aware of everything that is going on around you but will have no interest in it.

We call this state, "**Resting in the Spirit.**"

It can also be achieved by being prayed over by others who are with the Spirit; to say it as we do in the Charismatic movement.

This is another form of Prayer, which is a direct communication with Our God who is always with us. A very Holy Place to be!

You ask, "How is this useful, and how do we apply it to ourselves to accomplish anything? Well, it is a State of Grace in which many good things can happen.

The Spirit Of Fire

The Holy Spirit, the **Third Person of God**, is exhibited in various ways. During **Pentecost**, the Flames came down on the Apostles and they began speaking in Tongues in various languages. They now had new courage to Proclaim the Word of God, and began doing this immediately to the large crowd gathered there.

When we receive the Spirit, we are Changed, by God, and for His Purposes. We **Become a New Person**. Our purpose in life is changed, and we become an advocate for God.

Release Of The Holy Spirit

When we are conceived, as God the Father gives us His design for our body and nature, He also gives us a portion of His Spirit. When we are baptized in His Name, we become His own by our own choice, or by someone acting on our behalf, such as our parents.

When we make the personal choice to devote our entire existence to God, we are given gifts of the Holy Spirit, such as the gift of a personal, intimate relationship with Jesus and there are many Holy gifts that come with this. The Holy Spirit determines the specific gifts that are appropriate for the time, the person, and the place. Additional gifts may come with personal experience with The Lord, Jesus.

The Holy Spirit Consists Of:

- <u>Understanding</u> of All
- <u>Knowledge</u> and
- <u>Wisdom</u> with
- His <u>Power</u> and
- <u>Love</u> for
- Everybody and Everything Which
- God Himself Created!

Do not Neglect the Power of this Message!
We must <u>Believe</u>!

Focus On God Continuously

Practice <u>Silence in Solitude</u> with Focus on Jesus, The Father, and The Holy Spirit.
Let Him Come to You! "Wait on Him!"
The More Time we spend in this, will bring us closer and closer to Him.

Understanding Prophecy From God:
Release of the Holy Spirit

There are two distinct worlds in force here in our present time. There is the Kingdom of God which had its origin with Christ coming to earth, and the world of perception in which we live. The

Kingdom is truth and reality. The world we live in is based upon falsehood, spin and lies.

Prophecies may come from false prophets, but some may be real. We tend to interpret these literally but they must be understood in the context of the times and events which are presently occurring. It is like a code to be deciphered for understanding the message. Imposing prophesy from God in relation to our present world may be challenging and extremely difficult to comprehend the message.

God's messages are timeless and are always true but must be taken in context to what is happening around us to begin to understand what the message is telling us. Symbols are the usual mechanism as what we expect in reality is only a symbol of what is intended, and this in relation to our present world. The present world shifts and changes constantly and God's truth never moves.

God's Methods Of Teaching His Word

God teaches through His Church, "What Is Truth." His Spirit Teaches through His Messengers, "Why this is True."

Today Is All We Have

We cannot change the past, and we do not know the future. All we can do is our very best today.
"Jesus"

Lessons In Life

- **Assumptions** - Almost every one of our **Assumptions** is **Wrong**! We make most of our decisions based upon what we know based upon them. Since most of them prove to be incorrect, we spend a lot of our time changing our plans.

When Events Do Not Transpire As Expected

There is <u>Only One God and Creator.</u>
<u>He Created Everything that is Original.</u>
God either Causes Everything or Allows them to happen for His Purposes. He creates some good from every evil.

God constantly watches His Children, whom He has created Personally with much Joy and Glee. He allows them Free Will and He observes what they will do. God watches over us Constantly and knows every thought, word, and action we take. God is especially pleased when we follow the Direction He set for us at Conception, and as we take His Way as Our Way.

"It is only through True Love, which can only be active and valid if it comes by our Free Will."

God despises Hate and does not Tolerate it. His message is <u>Love is Everything</u>; the answer to all problems.

Everything Happens for a Purpose, His Purpose!

God's Love And Gifts To His Children

Sexual expression is part of God's Plan for His children. He desires that they have Pleasure in enjoying His Gift of Love. This results in new Life originating from enjoying each other in the Worship of God.

My Experience With God And My Father

One evening while I was sitting in our living room with my wife, I had an experience involving God and my father. My father is long dead and his spirit, I am sure, is in Heaven.

I was fully awake and my wife was in the room with me, probably reading. I was aware of everything that was going on around me. In my mind a very vivid vision came upon me. There was God the Father on my left in the middle of the room facing to my right. Directly in front of Him was my father, facing God. Now I didn't actually see my father, but his voice was so distinct that there is absolutely no doubt that it was him. I sensed his presence in my mind's eye. I did actually see God the Father but not with a lot of distinct detail of His features. The one outstanding feature was *He is Huge*, by human standards, far larger than a sumo wrestler. He was sitting down, but if He were standing I expect he would be over eight feet tall, and solid! I could not discern what they were saying to each other, but it was obviously about me. I did not hear any words from God, only from my Father.

This vision did not last very long, but it left me with a longing to know what it was all about and what this meant for me.

Satan's Agenda And Methods

- First, "I (Satan), do not exist!"
- Second, "There is no God!"
- Divide and conquer.
- Lie to us, "We are all the same." The Truth – Each of us is unique in talents, handicaps, and interests.
- Convince Us there is only one path to God.
- He can Take Words of Love and Consolation from One, and modify them into words opposite in meaning, to Sow Hate and Unforgiveness in another. Satan has this capability which can cause separation and desperation between individuals.
- Implement Disorder and Confusion.
- Promote All Lies, Destroy Truth.
- Etc., etc., etc.

There Is Only One God

Each of us was created by the One God! He Loves each and everyone of us as His Only Child!

He makes no distinction of where we have moved ourselves to in beliefs, but Jesus is His Son whom He placed here to tell us again, and reiterate His Truth as to how to Love Him, Be with Him, and Live for Him.

We are His! It makes no difference to God as to where we are, He takes us from there and moves us to where He Is, the Guiding Light! We must always focus on Him for Our Goal is to be with Him.

Many belief systems have been developed by us, or by Satan, which divide us and confound us in our pursuit of Our God and eventual salvation. The Catholic Church was established by Jesus while here on earth and passed over to apostle Peter, our first Pope. We must follow what Jesus taught, but, as sinners, we cannot do this perfectly. Therefore, we are all sinners and seek forgiveness.

Let us not be mislead by the evil one, and follow various belief systems; let us seek God instead.

There is, **<u>ONLY ONE GOD</u>**! Let us all seek and follow Him from wherever we are. He will lead us to Himself.

<u>Satan Controls Us Through What We Love</u>

One of the methods that Satan uses very effectively is to inflict on us doubts, concerns, and at times, severe suffering. To accomplish this, he selects the objects we love and care deeply about, and since we care, he has our undivided attention. He uses this technique to confuse, confound, and at times, destroy us.

Frequently, these doubts and concerns are carried by us for a very long time. The pain we carry is used by Satan to direct our thoughts and actions away from God and toward himself. He ties us up in his web of deceit which prevents us from serving God.

When we do gain control, and not let ourselves care about these things any longer, **We Become Truly Free**, and Satan no longer has this hold on us.

Therefore, the only answer is to seek God, and His Mercy, instead of remaining in the depths of despair that Satan inflicts upon us.

Let go and Let God handle our problems without fail. Then there are no opportunities for Satan to control our time and thoughts and actions. Trust in God, and he will never fail us.

<u>CONCLUSION</u>

It has been such a tremendous **Blessing to me** that I was selected by Our God to record and distribute these Messages.

I asked Him many times, "Why me, O God?" He always responded, "If not you, then who?"

None of these recorded Words are from me, they are directly from His Spirit.

They are intended to be heard, followed in obedience, and used to Glorify God.

I was given the subject matter while praying my daily Rosaries. I would have to stop, go to the computer, and take dictation. Initially I was not allowed to change any word, punctuation, or anything.

Later, with His Writings, He began to give me messages while I was not praying the Rosary.

I am honored to be His Scribe. When I was first called to His Church, He told me, "You are a Scribe and a Messenger."

I didn't know what that meant at the time. I know now! He uses me to give others His messages from time to time. Almost always, loving messages, but not always. Some are for corrections

This may be **Unique**. I do not know. There may be many others that God is using to spread His Holy Word. His Plan and Purpose is to bring all of His Creation back to Himself so we may be in His Kingdom with Him.

LET GO AND LET GOD

Release All Control To Him

FREDERICK G. MACKAMAN

CONTENTS

INTRODUCTION...59

Let Go And Let God...61
Our History In God's Grace.................................62
Accessing The Inner Self...................................62
The Man I Was Meant To Be..................................64
Hearing God's Voice..65
My Life Story of Miracles Begins...........................65
My Early Life..66
My Life In The Army..66
Understanding Unbelievers..................................68
For Healing Prayer...68
We Are All Control Freaks..................................69
God Is Always The Same.....................................70
In Heaven We Will Be All In One With God...................71

Conclusion To Let Go And Let God...........................72

INTRODUCTION

"I live for the **Word of God** and the **Teachings of Jesus."** These are **My Truths.**

These **Words** are from the Holy Spirit, the third person of God. They come to me primarily while I am praying my rosaries during the day. I either stop and write them immediately or place them on notes to be recorded later. I am assisted by the Holy Spirit with the wording when I write them.

I have been a Christian since 8-years old. I converted and became a disciple of Jesus in the Assembly of God Church during Daily Vacation Bible School. I was not baptized. I have lived according to the principles taught by Jesus ever since.

My birth mother died of influenza when I was 3-years old. In those days fathers did not raise their children independently. My dad was taking me to work with him and to restaurants to eat. I could not eat after my mother's death. In a restaurant my dad was trying to get me to eat. A young lady 19-years old said, "I can get him to eat," and she did. I immediately started calling her, "muvver." My dad hired her as a full-time housekeeper who lived with us. Not too long after this they were married. My dad was 44-years old. Many years later in my life, my mother told me that she married my dad so she could raise me. The first of many miracles in my life.

My dad died when I was 14-years old. He had divorced my mother when I was twelve, and I was living with him. The judge at the hearing granted custody to my mother's family as she had married again by this time. So, I stayed with my grandmother, grandfather, and two uncles. One of the uncles was an Assembly of God minister and ministered to the farm workers.

That was a perfect environment for a teenager to be in; a very spiritual family to show me how to live. I flourished, spiritually. Another major miracle.

In my several careers I have always been moved ahead of others and rewarded with so many gifts and achievements that it is truly amazing.

My entire life has been blessed with many miracles. I am certain everyone has similar experiences if they just recognize them.

This brief account of my life is to illustrate the background that I have been given by God to prepare me for the **Mission** He has given to me.

This **Mission,** which He told me when He brought me into His Church, the Holy Catholic Church which Jesus Founded, was to be, a **Scribe and a Messenger.**

This document was dictated to me by the Holy Spirit to convey God's Message to the world. Most of the revelations were given to me while praying my rosaries. The Holy Spirit has directed me to pray the entire rosary, 20-decades, every day.

I am so humbled that He would entrust this tremendous responsibility to me. When I ask God, "Why me?" His response is always the same, **"If not you, then who."**

Let Go And Let God

It has been revealed to me that when we "Let Go and Let God" take over, miracles can happen. Also, and this is important, we can experience events that normally happen only in Heaven.

Such as, being in one place and transferring to another at merely the thought of it. This is recorded in the Holy Bible in at least two places. When Jesus and the Apostles were in the boat, and the wind had just been calmed by Jesus, they were immediately transported to their destination.

Another instance was when the King's Treasurer had just been instructed as to what the Holy Readings meant, God's Instructor, which He sent to perform this task, was taken to his destination.

My experience is in Time. Place is just another manifestation of time. When I pray my Rosary and concentrate on each meaning of each stanza, I frequently am taken from the beginning of the decade to the last part. Some may argue that this is just my mind playing tricks on me, but this must be experienced to believe it.

Think of the experience of having a remote person take over your computer, cursor and all, when you allow this, so a problem can be corrected by the expert. This is the same experience as letting God take over our life temporally to solve our problem, hence, a miracle.

The key to allowing this to occur is we must "Let Go and Let God," We must totally let go of all our thoughts, feelings, and desire to retain control of ourselves! Otherwise, God cannot take over to satisfy our needs. We are blocking Him by demanding control over ourselves. He is dependent on us to "Allow" His Control of our self to affect His result.

This principle is in effect when we totally have no control of the result, and "Give Up." Then we are fully open to God's Grace to help us in our distress.

We must have an Open Mind and an Open Heart to Receive God's Messages and Assistance to accomplish what He has Planned for Us. We must Let Go of all Personal Feelings. Let Go and Let God take charge of your entire life.

This is what He requires to aid us, that we open ourselves to <u>Totally Depend Upon Him.</u>

Amen.

God is Magnificent!

<u>Our History In God's Grace</u>

Our God, the Only God, Created the Universe which is the size of a hazelnut in His Left Palm!

In His Creation He produced Beauty, Order, and All Love. When He had created all of this, He Marveled at the Wonder of it all. He was Much Pleased with His Work.

To Fully Enjoy this Creation, God needed some Creatures like Himself, to share in Appreciation of the Beauty and Magnificence of it all.

To satisfy this need, God Created Us, His People. He created us in His Image, and in His likeness. We are like Him in all respects, except He is Our God, and we are to Love Him and Serve Him. In His Spirit we are to Love and Serve each other also.

God created each one of Us as Unique individuals, no two alike, not even twins. He treats each one as an Only Child and is with each of us always.

As God created each one of us, He gave us many Gifts. He also gave us Free Will to do as we please. Therefore, He wanted to Test Us to insure we would follow His Instructions.

<u>Accessing The Inner Self</u>

There may be times in your life when you ask yourself, "What Am I Missing?" You feel incomplete and unsatisfied. No matter what you accomplish, you still need more. Peace in your soul is lacking.

God's Spirit is within us, and we activate it within us by accepting His Will in all things. Unless you have the Holy Spirit within you, you are missing the Best of Life, and Eternal Salvation.

The process of Accessing the Inner Self has not been understood. Many have pursued this goal for thousands of years.

It can be explained on several levels, 1) Physical, 2) Psychological, 3) Mental, 4) Spiritual, and there may be other ways.

I choose the Spiritual Way since I am more familiar with this as I am what is called, a "Charismatic Christian." What is this? It is striving to live according to the Way that Jesus instructed us to live. You may ask, how is this different than the traditional way that is taught by existing Christian Religions? The answer to that question is very simple; we attempt to live this Way to the very best of our ability, even though we cannot be perfect as Jesus was. We do not "Cherry Pick" what we choose to believe in; we take His Teachings seriously and follow them exactly as taught with no changes, additions, or deletions!

To get into the state of Oneness with your Spirit can be achieved in several ways. I choose to explain the way I am most familiar with.

Place yourself in a state of quiet, and alone from all distractions.

Relax -> "Let Go" -> Release of All thoughts and feelings -> Become Totally Open to God (Who is Always within Us.) -> Totally Surrender to Him - Retain Nothing for Yourself -> Giving Up All Control of Self – Only Open to God Himself.

You will feel nothing but perhaps Euphoria, or just Perfect Peace and **At One With the Word**. You will be aware of everything that is going on around you but will have no interest in it.

We call this state, **"Resting in the Spirit."**

It can also be achieved by being prayed over by others who are with the Spirit; to say it as we do in the charismatic movement.

This is another form of Prayer, which is a direct communication with Our God who is always with us. The Most Holy Place to be!

You ask, "How is this useful, and how do we apply it to ourselves to accomplish anything? Well, it is a State of Grace in which many good things can happen.

As you are praying for a specific item, visualize the action taking place, see it happening, or as it has happened, and claim it. Accept that it has occurred. Then claim it! Always thank God for His Deliverance, Goodness, and Mercy. Love God in your prayers.

The Man I Was Meant To Be

Why did I become someone else; someone other than who I was meant to be? I ponder and wonder the meaning of this conundrum. I did not plan to become who I turned out to be; it must have been someone else who planned it for me.

I have a faint dislike for myself, but that is who I am. I am the sum of all my wants, desires, and aspirations. Some are good, some are entirely selfish. I wonder who determines these things; is it me?

When I examine these thoughts of mine, especially under the focus of absolute honesty and truth, I am astonished! I am forced to ask myself, "Who am I, and where and when did I develop into this person that I have become?"

As I look back over my life, I had the utmost desire to become the very best that I could be. From where did this idea come, and how did it get into my head? I could answer from a strictly religious view, but that is too simplistic. I sincerely pursue the truth in this matter, as I attempt to do in all matters. Absolute truth is elusive.

What is truth? Who determines what is right and what is wrong? If we look to Our Creator to answer these questions, we get absolute answers. If we are True Believers in Him, we now have our answers. It is I, we, who have given ourselves the person we are. We have exercised our God Given Free Will of choices and arrived at this person of Who We Are!

Why am I not satisfied with Who I Am? I do not have full respect for others who exemplify certain characteristics which I have. We are all selfish to some degree. We want what we want, and we want it now. Of course, we are all human and this is our nature.

If we do not experience constant change, we are dissatisfied with our life and boredom is the result. We must continue to learn and to grow in knowledge and experience. Life is a process with no discontinuities. We must change and adapt to life's changes. We cannot remain the same. The real question is, "What must we change in ourselves?"

Hearing God's Voice

Let us begin with the hearing of The Lord God's Voice.

We hear voices in our head constantly, and we think they are our thoughts. There are only two sources of original thought. You may believe those are our thoughts, but they are not. We cannot generate something from nothing. Original thought is either from God, or from The Evil One, Satan. When questioned on this, God revealed to me the true test is, *"If the idea results in good, then it is from Me, if the results lead to evil, then they are from The Evil One."* This made sense to me.

We can take these thoughts and manipulate them with our own life experiences and come to any number of conclusions. Frequently, we mislead ourselves with our false reasoning. It is so easy to continue down this path with an active mind.

If you listen to God, Our Creator, He wants to Help us in everything, even down to the smallest details.

Let Him Help! Our God is constantly waiting for us.

My Life Story of Miracles Begins

Frederick Garland Mackaman - Born October 7, 1932

My birth mother died of pneumonia and childbirth when I was three years old.

My dad, at 44-years old, married a 19-years old girl/woman to take care of me. She told me years later she married him just so she could raise me. From the first time we met in a restaurant when I wouldn't eat, she got me to eat. I called her, "muvver." This was my new mother that God sent for me. **A miracle!**

A major **miracle,** and a very major turning point in my life.

My new mother's family were devoted Assembly of God Church people and were very humble, and spiritual in everything they did. For every major decision, they would meet as a family group and pray over the decision seeking the answer.

However, my new mother was a rebel and was not into that at all. She gave me all her love.

My Early Life

- My Life in the Army - 1953-1955 Always pushed ahead in leadership roles. Many **Miracles**.
- My Finding My Soul Mate and Companion
- My Work Career
- My Drinking Problem - Began with business trips, continued after that. Finally, one day, that just stopped! I didn't even notice I wasn't drinking that night. No desire. Major, major **Miracle.**
- Three years and two months before God's Call and baptism, is when I stopped drinking; my mind expanded tremendously as I was given the gift of understanding and suddenly, I could understand things I could never understand before. My hair had turned gray, and I was physically going downhill fast since retirement. Now this entire process was dramatically reversed, and I looked much younger. Even now, at 90-years of age, people cannot believe my age. I look like I am in my 50's! My mind is in my 30's.
- On Mother's Day, 2005, I had this life changing epiphany, which was called by God. A major **Miracle, a once in a lifetime experience.**
- Baptized September 26, 2005 Confirmed February 10, 2006.

I became a Charismatic soon after baptism. I have had deep spiritual experiences in Boca Raton and Bothell Catholic Churches.

God talks to me frequently, guiding me in what He wants me to do for Him and for His children.

My Life In The Army

I was called into the U. S. Army, and served during the Korean War at Ft. Lewis, Washington for 2-years. My mother prayed for me since all the basic training groups preceding mine, were sent directly to the front lines. My cycle of training was the first to not be sent directly there; we were disbursed to several different places. My mother considered this a **Miracle** and an answer to her prayer. Since I had applied for and been accepted as a candidate for Officers Candidate School (OCS), I was placed in the Division Replacement Company to await orders.

I experienced several **Miracles** during my tour of duty. In basic training all the squad leaders were replaced after the first 8-weeks of training. I was one of those appointed to replace those who were removed and to become a squad leader, which consisted of being responsible for eleven other individual soldiers in my squad. This was my first leadership role. I had all leadership positions after this. I consider this a minor **Miracle.**

I applied for Officer Candidate School (OCS) and was accepted to attend Artillery OCS which is the one I had selected, and I awaited orders until the next class was to begin.

While I was awaiting orders, the Army Base Division established a program to improve community relations with the local population. A competition was held to select the "Soldier of the Week." This was out of the entire division population of approximately thirty-five thousand soldiers. Much to my shock, and surprise, I was selected. This was indeed a major **Miracle.** Included in the planned rewards for this was an evening on the town of Tacoma, a new Pontiac to use, a date with the town beauty queen, tickets to a major show, and dinner at the best steak house. I also could bring a buddy and we had accommodation at the best hotel in town for the night.

As Soldier of the Week, I spent a week with the Post Commander, a One-Star General, and a week with the Division Commander, a Two-Star General. This General told me that every Division Commander had the prerogative of appointing two candidates to West Point each year. He offered me one of those positions! This was a rare opportunity for the competition for entry to West Point is tremendous. A special opportunity. A real **Miracle!** I politely declined the offer. I had already determined that the Army was not the life for me. I have always valued creativity and having tried it twice during my service interval, I found it to be totally unacceptable, to put it mildly. Taking orders exactly is the only mode that would be tolerated.

At a future point in my life I was hired by IBM, another **Miracle** for me, and they rewarded creativity!

Understanding Unbelievers

I have always had a great deal of difficulty understanding why some people cannot accept God's Word.

For me, it is so simple and fundamental. God cannot tell a lie, and by definition, His Word is True!

Most people probably accept this Truth; so why cannot they act on His Message to us? It is all a mystery to me; it seems so simple.

Another thing with unbelievers, especially atheists, "If they have not seen it, touched it, or tasted it or smelled it, or experienced it in some manner, it does not exist!" If they, personally, have not determined it exists, then they refuse to accept the new reality no matter the authority.

There is one caveat to this. If the new information supports their own agenda, then they accept it as real.

What we have not experienced with God, we cannot imagine! To appreciate God and what He offers to us, His children, we must have our own Personal Experience With Him.

For Healing Prayer

When we are praying over an individual for healing, there are options as to how to pray.

First, ask, "What do you wish to be prayed for?"

Next, ask them if you can touch them, and if you can use God's Prayer language, Tongues.

Then ask if they Believe they will be healed. This will test their faith. This is critical. They must believe, if not, pray for this Gift first.

Also, the person performing the Prayer must believe healing will take place.

Most effective Prayer Methodology, depending on the severity of the item being prayed for, is the following:

Lay hands on the person at the site of item being prayed for healing. Ask first.

Next, pray in tongues for further effectiveness. Again, depending upon severity. Again, ask first.

After Prayer is over, ask how they feel. Do they feel different in any way. Did they feel any heat in the injured part?

Healing may not happen right away, but it is common that it does happen at the time of prayer.

<u>We Are All Control Freaks</u>

Down deep in our soul we desire to control everything around us.

The reason it is a part of our nature is we want predictability in our lives. We detest and fear the unknown. We avoid it at all costs. When we do not know our future, we cannot plan for it and therefore are at the mercy of it, and it may contain danger to us and our kin.

That is why it is so difficult, and at times, impossible to change things which affect us.

To effect change we must educate and explain in detail all the implications of the implementation of the new way of doing things.

This applies to basic beliefs also, the most difficult of all to change. Religion is the prime example.

We think we are rational creatures. We are not! We are Emotional beings, and this is a good thing. It is mandatory for survival. When we recognize danger, we must react instantaneously. We must react to our," Gut Feel." Don't think, just act!

For us to accept God as Our Lord and Savior, it must be based on Trust; Trust in His Love for Us, and the Goodness of His Nature.

We cannot do this on our own. We must allow God to intervene and offer to us His Saving Grace, which He always holds out to His Children because He Loves His Creation so much.

It is so wonderful when we realize His offering of his Gift to us, and we trust Him and accept this life changing event which changes us forever.

<u>God Is Always The Same</u>

Our Lord is the Same Now as He Has Always Been! He Never Changes.

He can do whatever He wants in Miracles and in Changing His Laws which He Established!

Our God is Always in Charge of <u>Everything</u>! He either Makes Each Event Occur, or Allows it to Occur, for His Purposes!

God is not Limited by the physical laws of this universe which He established by His Creation. He can change them at any time He wishes for HIs Purposes, so let us not try to limit Him in our thinking and projection of what we expect Our God to accomplish. God has No Limits!

God creates Time for our benefit. He has no need for time as it is only a relational idea which refers to the movement of our planet, earth, in our solar system. He focusses on events and their relation to sequence of events. To gain perspective, this Universe is like a hazelnut in His Left Palm!

There is only <u>One Source for All Original Ideas</u>! That source is God, Our Creator, only He can Create! We are given these ideas to use in the development of everything we do. He allows us to manipulate these ideas and apply the results to accomplish what we wish to make happen.

Satan uses this same technique to manipulate these Original Ideas to accomplish the evil ideas he promotes within us.

There are only two sources for ideas in our conscious mind. God and Satan. We take these inputs and use them to develop our own thinking.

We are all Control Freaks! We want to know everything so we can control our destiny. Only God knows everything!

Our Love of God is what He Desires. We Love Him by Obedience to Him!

We live in this World which is not Reality, it is All Perception, our perception, not what is Truth, which is the True Reality. This world changes constantly; Truth never changes.

The definition of Truth is, "Truth Never Changes." It always remains the same and is repeatable. God's Word states the Constant, Real Truth.

Therefore, **Let Go and Let God** do everything for you. Depend upon Him in your planning, problem solving and in all difficulties. He is the source of our joy. **Let God resolve our issues for us and bring us the Joy that only He can bring.**

In Heaven We Will Be All In One With God

On earth we are born with God's Spirit within us, but we must activate it by choosing to obey it with our own Free Will. We choose Jesus by Baptism and Gain the Gifts of the Holy Spirit by Confirmation. These are accomplished by our own choice!

When we die and go to Heaven, we become All In one Spirit with God and All in Heaven. We retain our own Heavenly Body, which is a beautiful, glorified body.

On earth, before death, if we are obedient to God, our Spirit may reside with God in Heaven while it is with us on earth. We become one together.

<u>Conclusion To Let Go And Let God</u>

God is always with us. We must realize this to live a **Life in Christ.**

We must learn to feel His Presence.

To realize it, we must experience it.

To experience it we must **Let Go and Let God.** Totally surrender yourself during prayer and devotion. This is a dramatic experience in **Total Release of Self to God.**

Let go of everything; every thought, emotion, and feeling must be focused on God.

When we develop this capability, we will have everything we need to be One With God.

EVERYTHING HAPPENS FOR A PURPOSE

For God's Plan

FRED G MACKAMAN

CONTENTS

INTRODUCTION..77

My Mission - Given To Me By Our God.............................79
The Lord's Plan 80
God The Creator Is Always In Charge..............................80
God's Word Defined 81
Hearing God's Voice...81
HUMBLE YOURSELVES BEFORE ME.............................82
The Key Gifts Of The Spirit..82
He Is In The Eucharist 83
Beliefs In Holy Word And Occurrences...........................83
The Reason Many Have Left The Catholic Church............84
The Test For Satan 84
A Prophecy - For You 84
God Asked Me To Be Martyred.......................................85
My Visions 85
The Second Vision – Of God Our Father..........................86
The Third Vision – Of Jesus Petting Our Cat...................86
My Story 87
My Early Life 88
My Life Story of Miracles Begins....................................89

CONCLUSION – Everything Happens For a Purpose..............90

INTRODUCTION

<u>Everything Happens For A Purpose</u>

God has a purpose and Plan for everything! He has the power to alter His Plan at any time and for His Reasons.

We are to Obey His Plans as He makes them known to us! Obedience is how we display our love for him!

God is always in charge! He either causes events to occur, or allows them for His Purposes. We do not, nor can we understand His reasons; that is not our purpose. Our mission is to obey Him.

Satan was allowed to be the Prince of this world at the time of Adam and Eve, and used by God to test us for our obedience. We learn, and grow from our mistakes.

God's Goal is for all of His Children whom He Created, to know Him, seek Him, and devote themselves entirely to Love of Him.

There will be a Time for Reconciliation with God; we must be prepared for this at all times.

When Jesus Returns, He will return in Glory and will assume Control of this world. The faithful will be justified!

<u>My Mission - Given To Me By Our God</u>

When God first called me to His Church, the Holy Catholic Church, which was originated by Jesus with His Teachings while He was here on earth, He Told Me, **"You Are a Scribe and a Messenger."**

God has used me to write what He dictates to me, and He gives me specific messages for individuals at His request. I am highly honored to have been given this **Mission**. It is my greatest pleasure to Serve God in this manner.

One day while I was Adoring God in the Tabernacle where He is Kept, God told me, **"Pray the Entire Rosary every day."** This is 20 decades; It is the story of Jesus' Life.

While praying the Rosary, I am given thoughts and concepts. I must stop immediately, in the middle of the decade, go to my computer and **Write what God's Spirit Dictates to me!**

I cannot change a word, or the smallest part of the punctuation!

It is all **Words from God.**

That was only strictly applied to the first document God instructed me to write which is a 532 word list of **Teachings**, mostly just a modern rewording of Old Testament teaching brought up to date so and 7 year old could understand them. There are a couple of additions. One at the beginning which describes in detail the **Purpose of Life**. Another at the end which completes what happens at the end of Revelation.

God knows that this document must be reviewed and approved by the Church Fathers, which is a long process, at least 2 years. So, He instructed me to write my life story which incorporates some of these teachings. He stated, **"No one can debate, nor dispute what you have personally experienced."**

My life story became a long listing of many miracles in my life. In this document He began to allow me some flexibility in word and construction of sentences.

There are several follow on documents where God continues to dictate to me teaching from His Spirit.

The Lord's Plan

- God is Good, He is Perfect in Goodness
- God allows Trials to Test Us
- He helps us in Our Trials, especially if we ask Him
- We Suffer in these Trials as we All Suffer Trials in this Life
- He will never give Us anything beyond our capacity to endure
- Those who Persevere will Advance to Heaven
- There is no more Testing or Trials in Heaven
- Only Those who Have Endured will Be in Heaven
- We Will All Be Perfect in Heaven as God is Perfect

God The Creator Is Always In Charge

God is the Creator. There is none other. He created this Universe which is like a hazelnut in His Left Palm. This places us in proper perspective with God.

God, the Creator of Everything, remains in **Absolute Control of His Kingdom, Forever.**

God specified all the physical laws of this Universe, and has total control of them. He can change any part of His design whenever He desires.

We are so limited in our ability to think and imagine beyond our own lifetime of experience. God knows everything; **We Only Know What We Know.**

Everything that occurs, God Makes Happen! Nothing occurs without His Consent.

God Knows Everything! He makes Good happen from every disaster.

We do not think like Him, and He does not think like us.

He is Our Eternal God!

God's Word Defined

It is so simple! God is Love and the Source of All Truth.

God created all of us in His Love, For Love, so we can Love Him.

God desired Our Love for Him so He created us for that purpose.

For Love to be True Love, it must be given Freely so God gave us Free Will so we can Freely Choose to Love Him. Only this is True Love.

The reason God wanted us to Love Him Freely was so we can share in His Joy with His Creation, and in everything He does.

We are truly One With God. At inception God gave each of us His Spirit so we are all One With God, but He requires that we Choose Him Freely so our love is authentic.

The risk to God is if we do not choose Him, what will result? It could lead to disaster. Even though we have His Spirit and we are created in His Image <u>and</u> with His Spirit, this is new territory for him to explore. God created His Angels to Adore Him, but they do not choose freely. God wanted subjects who could directly share in His Divinity and experience the Joy with His Creations. We are them. Let us Rejoice and participate. Let there be no more reluctance.

To ensure that this experience would always result in Good, God established a Test Plan. Lucifer, being the Best and Highest Angel was chosen to be God's Test Vehicle. Satan, Lucifer, wa given the charge to do his best to test God's Plan to the worst case limits. He is doing exceptionally well.

Hearing God's Voice

Let us begin with the hearing of The Lord God's Voice.

We hear voices in our head constantly, and we think they are our thoughts. There are only two sources of original thought. You may believe those are our thoughts, but they are not. We cannot generate something from nothing. Original thought is either from God, or from The Evil One, Satan. When questioned on this, God revealed to me the true test is, *"If the idea results in good, then it is from Me, if the results lead to evil, then they are from The Evil One."* This made sense to me.

We can take these thoughts and manipulate them with our own life experiences and come to any number of conclusions. Frequently, we mislead ourselves with our false reasoning. It is so easy to continue down this path with an active mind.

If you listen to God, Our Creator, He wants to Help us in everything, even down to the smallest details.

Let Him Help! Our God is constantly waiting for us.

<u>HUMBLE YOURSELVES BEFORE ME</u>

Humble yourselves before Me.

It is My Will that is done.

Nothing occurs that I do not approve for my purposes. My plan is Sacred.

Do not question My Plans. Do not try to impose your desires upon Mine.

My Love applies to the good of All My Children.

<u>The Key Gifts Of The Spirit</u>

- **<u>Understanding</u>** - Of All of God's Messages
- **<u>Wisdom</u>** - To Apply the Understandings Appropriately
- **<u>Power</u>** - To Apply These Understandings Effectively

Normally given during **Confirmation**. But only if the Bishop/Priest has the Spirit; one cannot give a Gift One does not possess.

Can be given at any time by The Holy Spirit.

Person receiving this Gift must be Open to receiving it.

Can be Conferred by 2-who have The Spirit, by laying on of hands.

<u>People With the Spirit Recognize Each Other</u>

- Even at a distance, we recognize The Holy Spirit in the other.
- Frequently we Run to the Other and Hug Them, even before introduction.
- People with The Spirit have a Joy about them.

He Is In The Eucharist

Jesus has shown me that He Is in the Eucharist!

I told Him that I am a Believer and do not need to be shown His Truths.

His response was, "Oh yes, you must be shown all my work for no one can deny they exist if you have personal experience to relate. This cannot be debated!"

One time as were in our church in Florida praying, a little voice spoke to me saying, "Won't you come in front of me and kneel, and pray?" This was in front of the Tabernacle. I ignored it. Again, the voice spoke, but this time a little louder, "Won't you come in front of me and kneel, and pray?" I dismissed it again! Then the voice spoke, but this time in stentorian tones! "Won't you come and pray before me?" This I could not ignore; it was too real! So, I complied. At another time, He spoke, "Will you come and spend an hour with me?"

Adoration became my priority after that experience. I began to receive words of wisdom during adoration which I documented.

Later, God told me to pray the Rosary each day, which I did. After two weeks, He told me to pray the entire Rosary every day which I have done ever since. Revelations are given me while I am praying the Rosary.

Beliefs In Holy Word And Occurrences

We here on earth see, read, and hear of unusual events or occurrences and either believe them, or discount them.

It usually depends on whether we have personally experienced them or rely on a source which we have come to have a regard for their truth.

If the event, or information, does not meet with these criteria, we discount it. WE believe it does not exist!

Truth is hard to prove for some people.

Conditions in the world are constantly changing. Truth never changes. It is always the same. Science is based on repeatability of results. Even scientific facts change as we learn more about the subject being studied.

The truth that never changes is God's Word!

The Reason Many Have Left The Catholic Church

The Spirit of God, The Holy Spirit, is given at the time of Confirmation and Sealed into each Son and Daughter of God.

If the Bishop, or Priest administering this Holy Gift does not possess this gift, then He cannot grant what he does not possess.

This has resulted in many coming into the Holy Catholic Church not receiving this necessary Holy Spirit. Without this gift, we are exposed to the wiles and temptations of Satan and frequently leave the Church.

With this Precious Gift in our Hearts, Soul, Spirit and Mind, we will never leave our Holy Church!

The Test For Satan

Concern for Satan's words being in our mind, instead of Our God's Holy Word, is always present. I had been told that Satan can imitate God's Voice perfectly.

When I questioned this, a very spiritually filled friend gave me this advice. Test the input. Ask the voice: "Was Jesus born of the Virgin Mary?" He will have to answer truthfully, and that will be God's Voice.

So, I tried this approach at the next opportunity. Jesus answered, "You Do Not Test God!" He continued, "I Do Not Shout!" But Jesus followed with the True Test, "If the Message Results in Good, It is from Me, if It Results in Evil, it is from the Evil One!" That is the True Criterion.

A Prophecy - For You

God's Words For Me

You are a delight to <u>Me</u>! You are <u>My</u> own. Why are you concerned to prophecy? Just **Let Go.** Forget all thoughts, worries, and concerns about anything or anyone except for <u>Me.</u> Empty Yourself, totally! Rest in <u>Me.</u> Let <u>Me</u> Fill you with <u>Myself.</u> Then you will have <u>True Life.</u> I Love You So Much. <u>I</u> am <u>With You, Always!</u>"

God Asked Me To Be Martyred

- I Willingly **Agreed to be Martyred** when God ask this of me.
- He asked if I would **Surrender My Vision** so My Sponsor, Nigel, could receive his. After 2 years, I agreed!
- God asked if I would **Take On His Wounds for Him**. I declined.
- He is in the **Eucharist**.
- **Do not limit God!** Size of the Universe is like a Hazelnut in His Left Palm. He created All Physical Laws and can change them at His Will. Earth time has no meaning for Him; He can modify Time at His Will.
- Miracles are all around us!
- Mother Mary's Statue, recognizes us.
- My Wife, Charlotte's death and, Jesus and Mother Mary's participation.
- Everything Happens for a Reason!
- How God Designs Each of Us!
- There are **Many Paths to God,** and He Desires to Save Us All!
- God will **Not Deny Heaven** to any of His Children who desire to be with Him, and who Love and Obey Him.
- The Only Reality is God!
- **God is Love**!

My Visions – The First

I have been granted three visions thus far.

With the first one I was in Heaven. I was there as I had no sense of being on earth and I was awake and alive.

I was placed on a beautiful sloping hillside covered with flowing grass a foot long and rock boulders about five feet in diameter.

Sitting on top of the boulders and clustered on the grass around me were about 35-cats! They all were so happy to see me!

My intuition at the time was they were all the cats that I had petted in my lifetime. We were all ecstatic!

Later I surmised that the purpose of this vision was the following-

My youngest daughter, Cheryl, had recently lost her favorite cat to cancer. She was totally distraught. Her concern was that she would never see her cat again. After hearing this story from me, she was completely satisfied that she would see her cat again someday.

The Second Vision – Of God Our Father

I was in my apartment living area, sitting in my recliner, when I had a vision of God the Father sitting at the end of a long dining table.

At the opposite end of this table was a man whom I could not make out who it was. When he spoke, it was my father. He had such a distinct voice that there was no misunderstanding who it was.

I didn't understand their words, but they were discussing me.

What is so interesting in this vision of Our God. He was a large man, eight and a half feet tall husky in build, and swarthy in color. He was wearing a skimpy leather vest with no undershirt. I couldn't see his trousers.

I now know what the saying, "Fear of God" means. I was totally shaken with the enormity of being in the presence of God.

The Third Vision – Of Jesus Petting Our Cat

I was sitting in my recliner, facing, but not watching the TV.

Jesus appeared to the right front of my position, just a few feet away, faced to my left. He was sitting down and had our recently deceased favorite cat stretched out on a board on His left. Her name was Luv, and He was petting her with long strokes. He spoke to me, "You can come visit her anytime you want." I assumed that Jesus meant this after I was in Heaven. However, I have pondered this many times. Perhaps there may be a way I could visit Heaven with my desire to pet Luv.

My Story

My mother died when I was 3-years old. She died of pneumonia and was pregnant with an infant who was born dead upon her passing.

My father died of a heart attack when I was 14-years old. Even with these fateful events in my life, I have been blessed with many miracles by My God.

There are far too many to list, so I will only cover those with a major influence on my life.

After my mother's death I was with my father, and in those days, men did not raise children, women had this responsibility. While in a restaurant my dad was trying to get me to eat. A 19-year-old woman came over and said, "I'll get him to eat!" She did, and from that moment, I called her, "Muvver." My dad hired her as a housekeeper, and a few months later, they were married. My dad was 44-years old. Much later in life my mother told me that she married my dad just so she could raise me! A tremendous miracle, and life change for me. She was the major influence on me as I grew. That is, until my father divorced her when I was twelve, in order to be able to marry his female business partner who shared his high society interests.

Upon my father's death I was placed with my mother's parents and two brothers who were all very devout Assembly of God parishioners. In fact, one of the brothers was a Pastor of a congregation of farm workers. Both he and his brother frequently conducted revivals in nearby towns. He had purchased a huge tent, and a loudspeaker system for this purpose. Their entire family was poor as this was in the depression. They prayed as a family on any major decision they had to make. I witnessed them in this activity, and it was frequently in tongues. My grandmother had a huge influence over me. She would pray for healing on my scrapes and hurts, along with applying salve or other ointments. I would attend church with her on Sunday night as she preferred this service. My uncle, who was the minister, was ordained but had a day job. I learned my work ethic by observing him. On Sunday mornings, very early, I would go with him to the dairy where he worked. He worked 7 days a week. Later in life he became a full-time minister and no longer had to use the farm work-ers' meeting hall to conduct services. He was well liked and greatly respected by everyone.

This uncle, the minister, was named, "Joseph Elias Brand." He was short and his other brothers called him "Shorty." He hated this and I observed one time he and another brother fought in the weeds, rolling and scuffling over his being called this name. Another mira-cle, after forty years of age, he grew two inches in height!

Our God can do anything He wants, anytime He wants, and with any of his Favorite Children who Love Him so much! Miracles are common to those who Believe and Accept God's Love.

At eight years of age, I accepted Jesus as my personal Savior. This occurred at the Assembly of God Daily Vacation Bible School. The minister had all the boys kneel on the altar and pray for forgive-ness for their sins. I did this and accepted My God forever into my life. My mother was horrified as she was not religious, she and her younger sister were rebels. She felt that we had been taken advantage of as we now stated the pastor's directives in not going to movies, and in many other activities as they would lead to sin. Although I did not accept all of these, I lived my life according to what I was told was right by my grandmother and in my innate knowledge of right and wrong that had been given at my conversion experience. Even my entire family didn't know that I was now a Christian, I just lived as one. A major miracle wrought by My God.

My Early Life

- My Life in the Army - 1953-1955 Always pushed ahead in leadership roles. Many **Miracles**.
- My Finding My Soul Mate and Companion
- My Work Career
- My Drinking Problem - Began with business trips, contin-ued after that. Finally, one day, that just stopped! I didn't even notice I wasn't drinking that night. No desire. Major, major **Miracle.**

- Three years and two months before God's Call and baptism, is when I stopped drinking; my mind expanded tremendously as I was given the gift of understanding and suddenly, I could understand things I could never understand before. My hair had turned gray, and I was physically going downhill fast since retirement. Now this entire process was dramatically reversed, and I looked much younger. Even now, at 90-years of age, people cannot believe my age. I look like I am in my 50's! My mind is in my 30's.
- On Mother's Day, 2005, I had this life changing epiphany, which was called by God. A major **Miracle, a once in a lifetime experience.**
- Baptized September 26, 2005 Confirmed February 10, 2006.

I became a Charismatic soon after baptism. I have had deep spiritual experiences in Boca Raton and Bothell Catholic Churches.

God talks to me frequently, guiding me in what He wants me to do for Him and for His children.

My Life Story of Miracles Begins

Frederick Garland Mackaman - Born October 7, 1932

My birth mother died of pneumonia and childbirth when I was three years old.

My dad, at 44-years old, married a 19-years old girl/woman to take care of me. She told me years later she married him just so she could raise me. From the first time we met in a restaurant when I wouldn't eat, she got me to eat. I called her, "muvver." This was my new mother that God sent for me. **A miracle!**

A major **miracle,** and a very major turning point in my life.

My new mother's family were devoted Assembly of God Church people and were very humble, and spiritual in everything they did. For every major decision, they would meet as a family group and pray over the decision seeking the answer.

However, my new mother was a rebel and was not into that at all. She gave me all her love.

<u>CONCLUSION – Everything Happens For a Purpose</u>

God's Plan for us, His people, will be followed.

God's purpose for our journey here on earth is: We are being, Trained, Tested, and Prepared to be with God in Heaven forever.

God designed each one of us; we are unique; no two alike.

God treats each of us as His Only Child!

We cannot be made perfect as God is while here on earth, despite our best efforts. God's Grace and Mercy is required to forgive us and make us perfect as He is Perfect.

Those who do not adhere to God's Plan, well that is part of God's Plan also.

Final Conclusion to "An Anthology Of Christ's Teachings"

Writing this book has been a life changing experience for me. It taught me how Blessed we all are, to be the Creation of God, and loved by Him with a power beyond our imagination. He is always with us, and in us, as we are in Him. We have God's Holy Spirit with us constantly, and eternally to guide us in our quest to be like Him so we can be with Him in heaven forever.

This book consists of a brief sample of the behaviors required to achieve this goal.

There are many more of God's Teachings to be learned to be able to follow Him into Heaven; this book is just a small sample. We must never stop learning while growing in Him.

Each of us has our very own path, which is planned by God, and is constantly monitored by Him.

We are all Blessed by Our God.